Call the Witnesses

Perspectives on evangelism in

the Church of the Brethren

edited by

Paul M. Robinson

THE BRETHREN PRESS

ELGIN, ILLINOIS

Contents

Introduction

Wilbur Stover, a pioneer missionary for the Church of the Brethren, often declared, "Evangelism is the first great work of the church." While many are still inclined to agree with this priority of Christian responsibility, the commitment of local congregations to evangelistic efforts has often been inarticulate and uncertain.

The first decades of this century were frequently characterized by an emphasis upon mass evangelism. This was the era of revivalism at home and an expansive foreign mission enterprise abroad. With the changes that came through depression and war, social action and humanitarian service captured the imagination and determined the program priorities of many churches and their leaders.

Recent years have accented a growing concern among most congregations for a more effective Christian witness to the non-Christian community. This book is a symposium of perspectives on evangelism. The authors vary in their religious experience and in their theological insights. In spite of this diversity, a common acceptance of Jesus Christ as Lord gives evidence to a remarkable spirit of oneness among them. It is hoped that their testimonies will encourage the readers to call the witnesses to faith within their own Christian communities.

Paul M. Robinson, Editor

Paul M. Robinson *since 1953 has been the fourth President of Bethany Theological Seminary in Oak Brook, Illinois. He came to this position from seventeen years of service as a pastor, first at Ambler in suburban Philadelphia and for thirteen years at Hagerstown, Maryland. He was moderator of the Annual Conference in 1956 and was for many years a member of the General Board and its Executive Committee, serving for nine years as chairman of the Foreign Mission Commission. Paul Robinson's interests in cooperative Christianity have led him into active participation in the Maryland-Delaware Council of Churches of which he was for many years vice-president and in the Church Federation of Greater Chicago where he was for three years president. He has been a member of the Executive Committee of the American Association of Theological Schools. With Mrs. Robinson, he has traveled extensively, allowing him to preach on six continents and to visit more than seventy countries of the world.*

1

Call the Witnesses

Paul M. Robinson

I once served as the foreman of a grand jury. When we were seeking evidence in any case before us for decision, I was instructed to say, "Call the witnesses." It was the testimony of the witnesses that usually determined the outcome of the trial.

In the first paragraphs of his momentous book, *World History in Our Time*, Quincy Howe wrote, "The twentieth century has put the human race on trial for its life." I should like to paraphrase that sentence by saying, "The twentieth century has put the church on trial for its life." I do not mean that the purposes of God are at the mercy of the atomic bomb, the Kremlin, or the United States Senate. But the church, to whom God has entrusted the good news of his mighty acts in history, is going to be judged by the kind of testimony its members present to the world.

The gospel has proclaimed, "Jesus Christ offers hope for all mankind," and the world replies, "Call the witnesses." Christian theology has declared, "If any man is in Christ he is a new creation," and the world replies with the challenge, "Call the witnesses." The church has preached, "Christ brings salvation, healing and wholeness to both individuals and society," and the world, sometimes in desperation, pleads, "What is your evidence? Call the witnesses."

When Jesus, meeting for the last time in his earthly presence with his disciples declared, "You shall be witnesses unto me," he was uttering both a commission and a prophecy. The early Christians were scattered all over their world bearing witness to the truth that God had invaded the world through his son, Jesus Christ, and that there was no other name under heaven whereby men would find salvation. But they also gave testimony to what the presence of the living Lord meant to them, and declared that newness of life had been recreated in them by the power of his own resurrection.

These men and women had no special ordination as preachers and evangelists, except that commission inherent in their discipleship, yet they went everywhere fulfilling the Great Commission through their testimony. So, every Christian today stands in a kind of glorious apostolic succession, ordained by his baptism, like those first-century followers of the Master, to witness to the simple but powerful truth, "Jesus Christ is Lord."

And we cannot escape the truth that Christ is being judged today not so much by what he said as by what Christians say and do.

I was preaching in English one Sunday before a large congregation in Nigeria with the aid of an interpreter who translated what I said into Bura. I suddenly had a very irreverent thought, "How do I know that he is saying what I said?" Then I recalled a statement by the late Olin Downes, for many years music critic of *The New York Times*, "How tragically is every composer at the mercy of his interpreters." Superb as the music of Bach may be, he will be known to most people only by the skill with which his music is interpreted by other artists. With all his greatness as a playwright, Shakespeare in the hands of immature and incompetent performers may sound stupid and inane.

So is Christ, so often tragically, at the mercy of his interpreters.

The church must continually ask itself how faithful we are in our own witness to him whom we call Lord and Savior. How diligent are we in keeping evangelism, the first great work of the church, central to our congregational mission? We readily agree that the gospel is good news, not just for modern man, but for every generation, since it speaks to the heart of the human condition. A compelling motivation for evangelism lies in the conviction that Christ brings salvation, healing, and wholeness to life that without him is lost. The words of Peter in his witness to the religious leaders of his day still ring with compelling urgency, "There is salvation in no one else, for there is no other name under heaven given among men by which we must be saved" (Acts 4:12).

Christians, therefore, witness to good news about God. The poet, W. H. Auden, called ours the "age of despair." Events in the news every day contribute to a general feeling of discouragement and disillusionment which characterizes so much of our life today. But the good news declares that God still reigns and his purposes will surely be worked out in the destiny of mankind. In the glorious words of Maltbie Babcock, "Though the wrong seems oft so strong, God is the Ruler yet." Here indeed is hope. Hope does not deny the reality of evil. It simply reminds us of the fact that there is another dimension in the life of man which makes a profound difference in his outlook. God still holds the world in his own hand.

Carl Bratten, a Lutheran theologian, in his book, *The Future of God*, sums it up in this way, "Hope is not a denial of the facts, but a refusal to accept them as the court of final judgment. Likewise, a theology of hope takes evil seriously, precisely by anticipating a power that can more than match it. Hope counts on new possibilities which have not yet solidified into the core of established experience. Hope is on the lookout of something really new, and will not model the future on the past and present. It is hope that keeps alive the creative spirit of man."

This word of hope is central to the evangelistic witness of the church. God reigns, and God cares. In a world in which the individual too often feels nameless and faceless, God has a profound concern for every person, great or small. Christian evangelism proclaims, "God loves you," but a tired and skeptical world is saying, "Call the witnesses."

The gospel is also good news about man. This indeed is significant since most of the news about man is not good. Every day brings its own new evidence of man's inhumanity and corruption. Nor does the Christian faith deny this depravity.

There have been times when in the name of moral optimism some Christian theologians took their text from the third chapter of Pollyanna and seemed to promise that "every day in every way we're getting better and better." This unrealistic assessment of man was in truth a betrayal of the biblical understanding of human nature. It was a theology in which, as Richard Niebuhr so vividly put it, "A God without wrath, called a man without sin, to a kingdom without judgment, through a Christ without a cross."

The theological reaction to this shallow optimism went to the other extreme and tended to regard man as totally evil and incapable of any good. Some neo-orthodox theologians who were quite influential for a time, while affirming the spiritual bankruptcy of man seemed to overlook what man could become by the power of God's redeeming grace. In celebration of the total otherness of God and the transcendence of his purposes beyond human endeavors, they ignored the fact that in every age God has chosen to accomplish his will through the insights, skills, and commitments of those who are dedicated to him.

One of my professors of theology used to say, "When you think of the nature of man, you must remember two things: no man is as bad as he might be; and no matter how bad a man may be, the image of God is still within him, and he can be brought back into a restored relationship with his creator. He can be saved."

So the gospel does not simply see man as he is, weak and sinful and lost. It affirms what man can become by the recreating power of Jesus Christ. In a familiar and well-loved hymn, Isaac Watts wrote,

> Alas! and did my Savior bleed, and did my
>   sovereign die?
> Would He devote that sacred head for such
>   a worm as I?

In *The Brethren Hymnal*, the last phrase has been changed, and I believe helpfully, to read: "For sinners such as I." Whatever else he is, man is not a worm. He is a wretch and a sinner, but he is still a man. God would not send his son into the world to die for a worm. Christ would give his life for a man. That is good news. Whatever he has been, man can become a new creation by God's grace. Christians affirm this and our evangelism proclaims it, but a weary world replies skeptically, "Call the witnesses."

THE GOSPEL is also good news about Jesus Christ. The depth of God's love for the world is revealed in his willingness to send his own son to be its Savior. That is the heart of the Christian message. It is the central truth in Christian witness.

Read again the book of Acts. Here is the account of the ministry of the first-century church which was launched by the power of the Holy Spirit out of profound conviction that the resurrected Lord was the only hope for mankind. These early Christians clearly believed that without Christ the world was lost. It is terrible to be lost. Whatever is lost is not where it ought to be. In the parables of Jesus, the sheep was lost when it was not with the flock, the coin was lost when it was not in its owner's possession, a prodigal son was lost when he was not in the father's house.

The gospel recognizes that though he was made for relationship with God, man has been alienated from his Creator because of his own sin. He is therefore spiritually no longer where he should be. He is lost. But God sent his son to seek the lost and by the power of his own life and death and resurrection to establish a new relationship with himself. Thus, the wholeness and completeness which sin had denied can now be restored in a new quality of life. This is what the church calls salvation. Without this salvation, the spiritual health and healing which comes through the redeeming ministry of Christ, man is lost.

Concern for the lostness of both men and institutions unless they are brought into the purposes of God by Christ must be at the heart of Christian evangelism. No lesser motive will suffice. The desire to increase the membership of a congregation, the hunger for a wider human fellowship, the need to strengthen the institutional church, may all have values which should not be denied. But no one of these is the ultimate compelling reason for evangelism. When Christians share the conviction of the early church that Christ indeed is the hope of the world and without him there is no salvation, a desperate sense of urgency gives a new dimension to the witness of the church.

SINCE THE gospel brings to the world such hope and promise about the God who declares his love for man, and the reality of his salvation through Jesus Christ, the church must take with much greater seriousness her central task of witnessing to this good news. A truly effective church will understand that evangelistic witness must be at the heart of its ministry. It is a constant and continuing concern — not only when it seems appropriate to seek new members for the church. Indeed, the very life of the church is in her witness. The structures by which the congregation organizes itself for mission must, therefore, provide for a vital and comprehensive program of evangelism if the church is to be faithful to her purpose.

We are continually giving a testimony to the world — consciously or unconsciously. The word we speak for Christ is significant whether it appears in a sermon or in a personal encounter. But Brethren have also been keenly aware of the witness of life itself. A style of life that embodies the spirit of Christ, that gives evidence of concern for another's need, that reveals a personal commitment to the priorities and values inherent in Christian discipleship — such a testimony often speaks far more convincingly than any theological argument.

A man once came to see me as a pastor and asked how he might become a Christian and a member of my church. "For five years," he said, "I have worked with George who is a member of your congregation. I have never known a man who so completely lives what he believes and who is so thoroughly happy in his relationship with other people. He has something in his life that I want. George says that *something* is a *Someone*. I want to know Christ too."

If it is true that the church is on trial for its life in this half of the twentieth century, I have no fear that we shall fail through lack of skill in organization or even in the way we celebrate our faith. The test will come in our ability to communicate the gospel clearly and persuasively to a world that desperately needs God's saving grace.

God's power is sufficient. Christ's salvation is available to all. Mankind can be redeemed. This is the good news entrusted to the faithfulness of the church, and the world is waiting to hear it. "For the creation waits with eager longing for the revealing of the sons of God" (Romans 8:19). When the world cries, "Call the witnesses," let us be quick to respond as did the disciples so long ago: "We speak what we have seen and heard, and what we know because of him who is our hope and the hope of the world."

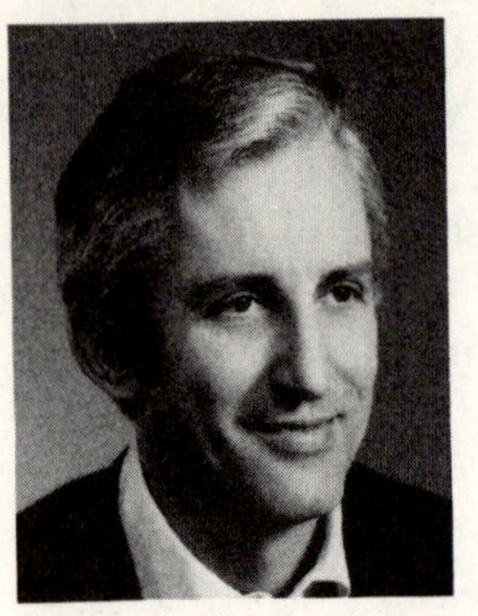

Vernard Eller *is probably the most prolific and best-known writer in the Church of the Brethren. His books range in reader appeal from a scholarly dissertation on Kierkegaard to comments on "The Mad Morality," viewing the Ten Commandments as seen through the eyes of Mad magazine. He is best known for his profound theological insights, interpreted from the perspective of the Anabaptist tradition in popular language and often with a delightful sense of humor. He has been a frequent contributor to The Christian Century. Now professor of religion at La Verne College in California, Vernard Eller was formerly editor of youth publications for the Church of the Brethren. He has also been a member of the summer faculty of the Pacific School of Religion. He is an active member of the La Verne Fellowship Church of the Brethren where he worships with his wife and three children.*

Go, Tell It on the Mountain

Vernard Eller

O thou that tellest good tidings to Zion,
*   get thee up into the high mountain!*
O thou that tellest good tidings to Jerusalem,
*   lift up thy voice with strength;*
*   lift it up; be not afraid!*
Say unto the cities of Judah,
*   Behold your God!*
Arise, shine, for thy light is come;
*   and the glory of the Lord is risen upon*
*   thee!*

A writer often leads off with a little story to catch the attention and interest of the reader. I propose to do better than that and use an *anthem* to lead into my sermon. It will call for a little cooperation on your part. If you have a recording of Handel's "Messiah," now find the alto aria based upon the words printed above and listen to it. If not that, get the score and sing it. If not even that, read the words above and hear in your head as much of Handel as you can. Our treatment necessarily will focus upon the *word* of God; but I am utterly convinced that God meant *those* words to be heard to Handel's music — it adds!

The composer's text is taken from two widely separated passages — Isaiah 40:9 and 60:1 — and uses a translation that does not conform even to the King James and almost certainly is in error. It seems clear that the prophet's original command was for *Zion* (Jerusalem) to get up into the high mountain — which is where it is located — and tell the good tidings to the lower down cities of Judah. Besides, neither we nor Handel will interpret the good news as the prophet intended: he was talking about the return of the exiles from Babylon; we are talking about what God has done in Jesus Christ. But all these glaring discrepancies will bother us not a whit; the Holy Spirit acts with a freedom that sweeps right over them!

O thou that tellest good tidings. "Good tidings" is, of course, a precise translation of our word "gospel" and the "evangel" of our word "evangelism." Yet perhaps we need to be reminded of the translation more often than we are; the gospel of our evangelism dare never, in the first place, be the conviction of sin, the threat of eternal punishment, or the implication of moral or spiritual distance between the evangelist and his hearer. No, always, in the first and primary place, we are called to be tellers of *good* tidings.

And once a person has "good tidings," once he is convinced that what he has *are* indeed "good tidings," what possibly is there to do about it except to "tellest" them? That's what good tidings are good *for;* that's about the only thing one *can* do with them. As a medieval English poet shrewdly observed, the likely reason God engineered a group of women to be the first discoverers of Jesus' resurrection was that he wanted the good tidings to be *told abroad.* Good tidings — truly *good* tidings — as much as impel their own telling.

It follows (inevitably, I am afraid) that to the extent we are not involved in some sort of evangelism, to that extent is indicated the fact that we have not yet heard Christianity as truly being "good tidings," the best possible tidings. The first step in evangelism, then, lies not in our deciding to become evangelists but in our hearing the gospel in such a way that nothing can *stop* us from becoming evangelists. Once the word actually is heard, it has its own way of making an evangelist out of the hearer.

In this regard, it must be said that the good tidings with which we are concerned are themselves broad enough and "good" enough that "evangelism" cannot be limited to signify only that proclamation directed at winning people to a first acceptance of Jesus. No, these tidings also are good for those who already know him as Lord and Savior. They are good for those who are still too young to adequately understand what it means for him to be Lord and Savior. They may even have a quality of goodness that can be heard by those who have chosen not to hear that he is Lord and Savior.

Although the telling of good tidings dare never *omit* the interest in new acceptances of Christ, neither dare it be *confined* to this interest. Yes, Christian education, worship, fellowship, and service — any activity that effectively communicates to anybody any aspect of the good news of what God has done for us in Christ is authentic evangelism. We need take care only that our pursuit of one sort of evangelism does not become an excuse for ignoring other sorts.

Get thee up into a high mountain; lift up thy voice with strength! The prophet seems to have had two thoughts in mind behind this command. First, Zion should get up to where she has a good angle for beholding God as he brings the exiles home across the Arabian Desert. An evangelist is not encouraged simply to charge out and start telling whatever he has heard from whatever source; he has a responsibility to *know* what he is talking about, to have seen it for himself with some clarity and perspective. So, get thee up into the high mountain of Bible reading and theological study, of learning what Christianity is, so that there will be some chance that the good tidings you tell will be an accurate report.

Second, obviously Zion should get up so that

her voice can be heard as far as possible. For us, this means that we should look out to find the methods and styles of evangelism which, *according to our own particular gifts and resources,* will make for the widest and most effective hearing. So what is *your* high mountain? For some, certainly, that which goes under the name "visitation evangelism." For others, perhaps, "revival preaching." For others, "everyday witnessing." For others, teaching. For others, writing (my own particular mound). For others, the providing of financial support, building up a high mountain from which someone else's voice can be heard. It would be foolish for us to try to enumerate all the possibilities. And it is foolish, too, for any evangelist to claim that *his* method marks the only truly *high* mountain and so look down on those who feel they can do better from a different peak.

Say, "Behold your God!" Here is perhaps the most important and helpful note of all. The message of evangelism can be summarized just this briefly: Behold your God!

"Look! Look! God is here! He has come to us in Jesus Christ! Look! See him in his love, his grace, his kindness, his helping and healing, his serving and saving! Behold your God; see *who* he is and *what* he does. See him come to you, come for you, come wanting you." Evangelism is more of a pointing and saying, behold — so that the other person can see for himself — than it is like anything else.

This means that evangelism is not a case of matching wits with another person, of trying to convert or win him (in the sense of "getting victory over him"). We simply invite him to look . . . and God is able to take it from there. This means that we do not in any sense make ourselves a focus of attention; we are pointing *away* from ourselves. We do not set ourselves over the other person to lecture him, to set him straight, to get his theology corrected, to sell him a product, to convince him he's a sinner, to get him to confess to us or to make a commitment to us or to sign a dotted line for us or to agree with us. No, simply: "Behold your God!" — calling his attention to God in as winsome a way as possible . . . and letting God take it from there.

In actuality God is his own evangelist — and an entirely capable one, it should be said. It is not that he has laid upon us the evangelism assignment as some sort of task that he needs us to do for him. Rather, he has invited us, offered us the *privilege* of joining *him* in the exciting thing he is doing. And all we are asked to do is point, "Behold your God!" — and if his beholding of God doesn't convince that other person, then you can be sure that none of your techniques would change the situation in any case. If you feel "a burden to win souls" (to expose an old chestnut of a phrase), it isn't *Christian* evangelism you're talking about, because it, by nature, is very much a light, free, exciting, "looky-here-would-you" sort of thing.

Arise, shine, for thy light is come! This is it, what evangelism is all about! Rise and shine! And you don't even have to generate your own candle-power. The text makes it clear that the only reason you *can* shine is because thy light is come and the glory of the Lord is risen upon thee. Your shining is done with *reflected* light and in no other way.

Each morning when the sun comes up and its first rays hit the snow-crowned top of Old Baldy (the ten-thousand-footer beneath which I live), what does it do? It rises and shines. "Rises?" Indubitably; any fool can see that that mountain is much higher early in the morning than at any other time (you can't even see it after the smog builds up). From its high mountain, Old Baldy gives a witness and tells to the cities of Judah (actually, of the eastern Los Angeles basin) the good tidings that the sun is up and the day has come. Behold your God!

And now that the Sun of Righteousness has risen upon *us,* what are we to do? Obviously, arise tall and proud and free — and *shine!* And just how does one do that? There are as many different ways of doing it as there are different people. Don't let anyone tell you that it has to be done a certain way or it isn't evangelism. No, you let the light shine in the way it happens to bounce off a "you"-shaped mountaintop — whether that happens to be an Old Baldy or some more hirsute prominence. If the light is indeed that of the glory of the Lord, the shape of the reflector won't make all that much difference. It is all right, even, to plan, learn, and practice some "evangelistic techniques"; but it is not here that success or failure lies. The only success is the success that God himself gives to the effort; the only failure is the refusal to rise and shine.

How varied can they be, these ways of evangelism, of telling the good tidings? We will speak to the question through our closing hymn. Recall our opening anthem and what Handel did with the Isaiah texts through the use of classic, formal, sophisticated orchestration. But hear now (better, *sing* now) another treatment of one of the same texts, exploring the same idea, proclaiming the same message — yet done in a completely different musical idiom. And don't you even dare ask the question as to which is the truer, more authentic expression. If it is the one God they move men to behold, both are wanted and both needed.

> *Go, tell it on the mountain,*
> *Over the hills and everywhere.*
> *Go, tell it on the mountain —*
> *That Jesus Christ is a-born!*

The best news comes to us in Jesus Christ. . . . To a struggling humanity, Jesus Christ brings home the truth: We are delivered! Turn toward the light! Let us grow! In shadows of despair the Word comes clear: "Rise, pick up your life and run. I am running with you."

From: *A Statement on Evangelism,*
Annual Conference, 1972

Harold S. Martin *has success-fully combined a career as junior high school mathematics teacher with his ministry to the Pleasant Hill Church of the Brethren near York, Pennsylvania. He is known to many as chairman of the Brethren Revival Fellowship, and has conducted more than seventy evangelistic campaigns across the Brotherhood. He has represented the Church of the Brethren as an observer to the convention of the National Association of Evangelicals. Harold Martin has also served his denomination on several study committees, and was a member of a task force to plan special events for his district in their cooperation with the Key '73 emphasis. He has written extensively for several religious journals, has been a contributor to church school lesson publications, and is the author of* Sermons on Eternal Themes.

Make Known the Message: the Biblical Basis

Harold S. Martin

Brethren have always laid strong claim to a biblical basis for their doctrinal stance and their church function. We maintain that the New Testament is our creed, and the New Testament has much to say about evangelism.

Brethren have historically maintained a strong evangelistic thrust. Alexander Mack and Christopher Hochmann went up and down the Rhine Valley in Germany, preaching the gospel of Jesus Christ. It was the continued interest in evangelism that made possible our phenomenal growth in the United States. Early Brethren moved to new frontiers and established churches wherever they went. Donald Durnbaugh says in *The Church of the Brethren Past and Present*, "In the autumn of 1724 the entire male membership (fourteen in number) of the Germantown congregation set forth on an evangelistic tour in the wilds of 'Penn's Woods.' Their expedition led to the formation of two new congregations." Over the years Brethren have had an interest in evangelism.

The very nature of our biblical understanding — and of our view concerning the mission of the church — prompts us to believe that God's people should be continually winning more people to faith in Jesus Christ.

THERE ARE many ideas about the meaning of evangelism. To some, evangelism is what Billy Graham does and what their pastor does not do. To others, evangelism is firing a stream of Bible verses at prospective converts. To still others, anything one does as a Christian is evangelism.

The Bible does not give a quick answer when we search for a definition of evangelism. The word *evangelism* in fact is not in the Bible — but the words *evangelist* and *evangelize* are there, and from these we learn what evangelism is. The Greek word *euaggelizo* means "to preach, to proclaim the good tidings, to tell the good news." The angels evangelized. They brought "good tidings of great joy" (Luke 2:10). Jesus evangelized.

He preached the "glad tidings of the kingdom of God" (Luke 8:1). Paul evangelized. He said, "I have preached to you the gospel" (2 Corinthians 11:7). Philip evangelized. He "preached unto him Jesus" (Acts 8:35). Evangelism in the Bible, then, was a ministry of the spoken word. Evangelism means "to make known the message of the gospel."

Evangelism is not the mere testimony of a good, consistent life. The quiet, pervasive influence of the Christian life is necessary — but it is not evangelism. Being friendly, helpful, and neighborly may be a necessary *preparation* for evangelism, but it is no *substitute* for evangelism. Christianity cannot be radiated; truths about God and his son have to be communicated. Good deeds do not convey the actual content of the gospel; the good news must be expressed in words. Evangelism, then, is the specific, articulate presentation of the message that Christ's death upon the cross propitiates (turns away) God's wrath which abides upon man in his unregenerate state (Romans 3:25; John 3:36). Evangelism is the presenting of Jesus Christ, so that men will accept him as their Savior from the guilt and power of sin, and declare him Lord as they seek to follow him in their daily lives.

C HRISTIANS are motivated to share the good news primarily because our Lord *commands* us to evangelize. The heart of the Great Commission in Matthew 28:19-20 is "Go therefore and make disciples of all nations." The command in Acts 1:8

is "Ye shall be witnesses unto me." At the Berlin Congress on Evangelism John R. W. Stott said: "We engage in evangelism, not necessarily because we want to or because we choose to, or because we like to; but because we have been told to. The church is under orders. The risen Lord has commanded us to go, to preach, and to make disciples, and that is enough for us."

We are motivated to evangelize also because men are lost (Luke 19:10), without hope (Ephesians 2:12), under condemnation (John 3:36), and destined for destruction (Mark 16:16). For some, nobody is lost in the eternal sense; nobody is really perishing; nobody is destined to spend eternity in hell. This is a new form of an old universalism — but Jesus taught eternal punishment as well as eternal life (Matthew 25:46).

There is an estrangement between man and God which needs reconciliation (2 Corinthians 5:19). Jesus says that it is sin that defiles us and cuts us off from God (Mark 7:14-23; cf. Isaiah 59:12). Something happened in the Garden of Eden that blighted the entire human race (Romans 5:12). As a result the whole human family is spiritually dead (Ephesians 2:1) and is under the grip of sin (Galatians 3:22). Therefore man needs to be shown the depth of his depravity and the extent to which he has fallen short of the expectation of God.

Francis Schaeffer in his book, *Death in the City*, discusses the question, "What would you do if you met a really modern man on a train and you had just an hour to talk with him about the gospel?" Schaeffer says, "I would spend forty-five or fifty minutes to really show him his dilemma; to show him that he is even more dead than he thinks he is; that he is morally dead because he is separated from the God who exists. Often it takes a long time to bring a person to the place where he understands the negative. And unless he understands what's wrong, he will not be ready to listen to and understand the positive."

The evangelist, then, is motivated by the bad news that every person in his natural state is a fallen, sinful creature who stands in need of a complete transformation. He knows that sin has brought God's displeasure, and "knowing therefore the terror of the Lord, we persuade men" (2 Corinthians 5:11).

The doctrine of the return of Christ has also been one of the great motivating factors in evangelism. The day of salvation is "now" (2 Corinthians 6:2). Jesus said there is a night coming "when no man can work" (John 9:4). The second coming of Jesus Christ is the blessed hope of every believer (Titus 2:13), and to desire others to share in that hope becomes an impelling motive for evangelism.

THE EVANGELISTIC message is centered uniquely in a Person — the Lord Jesus Christ. He is the way and the truth and the life. The scriptures say that when Philip the evangelist encountered the Ethiopian eunuch, he "preached unto him Jesus" (Acts 8:35). Paul's own testimony to the church at Corinth was: "For I determined not to know any thing among you, except Jesus Christ, and him crucified" (1 Corinthians 2:2). Paul was thoroughly trained in the school of the Torah at Jerusalem, and well versed in Hellenistic culture as a result of his training in Tarsus — but his one and only concern was to bear witness to Jesus Christ and his death upon the cross for the sake of all people.

The evangelistic message offers a remedy for man's alienation from God. The good news is that the death of Jesus has become a bridge between a holy God and a sinning people (1 Timothy 2:5-6), and that his blood propitiates God's wrath for those who accept him with a saving faith. The writer of Hebrews says, "So Christ was once offered to bear the sins of many" (Hebrews 9:28). Jesus himself said, "For this is my blood of the new testament, which is shed for many for the remission of sins" (Matthew 26:28). Romans 3:25 says of Jesus Christ: "Whom God hath set forth to be a propitiation through faith in his blood, to declare his righteousness for the remission of sins."

The good news is that we sinners do not have to die eternally since Jesus Christ died for us. The New Testament uses three prepositions when speaking about Christ's death: *peri* — for us; *anti* — in place of us; and *huper* — in behalf of us. Christ died for us, in place of us, and in behalf of us. The evangelist makes much of Christ's death upon the cross. The message of evangelism is that man is lost, undone, and without hope — but that Jesus Christ acted in our behalf by his death, burial, and resurrection (1 Corinthians 15:3-4). Christ took upon himself the penalty rightly belonging to us, so that through believing in him, we are freed from the penalty and guilt of sin.

Jesus offers pardon and forgiveness to all who receive him through faith (Acts 14:38-39), repentance (Acts 2:38), and baptism (Mark 16:16). One who accepts the new life in Christ, submits to him as Lord. Hate is transformed into love; selfishness into sacrifice; and pride into humble dependence upon what God has done for us. Homes are changed. Money is spent for that which is bread. Barriers that alienate men from one another are broken down. The new man in Christ has turned from the power of Satan to God, and becomes as salt to the earth.

THE NEW TESTAMENT illustrates several methods of evangelism. We find examples of mass evangelism in the work of John the Baptist, Peter, and Stephen (Acts 2:14-41). We see personal evangelism by observing the thirty-five personal interviews of Jesus as recorded in the Gospels (e.g., John 4:5-42). Paul used dialog evangelism on Mars Hill in Athens (Acts 17:16-34). The early Christians practiced visitation evangelism when they went from house to house as recorded in Acts 5:42. And then there was literary evangelism as seen in the writing of the Gospels of John and Luke (John 20:31).

The most common and perhaps the most effective biblical method of evangelism is the sharing of the good news on a person-to-person basis as we come in contact with others. Sometimes just being a friend or listening to another person's troubles becomes a point of contact. It is usually best not to pounce upon a prospect and start off on him. It is best to wait for an opportunity to open. Some think we should give the unbeliever a "believe-it-or-be-damned" ultimatum, but witnessing is relating to persons, and people have feelings. We need to take their feelings into consideration.

Traveling home from Chicago on a plane, I sat beside a man who seemed to be lonely. I asked him if he had been on a business trip, or visiting relatives, or if he objected to sharing the purpose of his trip. He told me about it; we had a general conversation; and then he noticed that I was reading Billy Graham's book *World Aflame*. At about the same time, the pilot informed us that we were approaching thunderstorms and seat belts were to be fastened. God used that thunderstorm and the title of the book to provide an opportunity to share the Christian faith with a needy soul. If you have ever been on a plane flying above thunderstorms, you'll never forget it! My partner sat there and listened to what was being said, like a little boy in Sunday school.

Sometimes a wisely chosen tract can be used as a good point of contact. Hand the tract and say, "Here's something that I'm sure will help you — I hope you can read it sometime." There is probably not much value in standing at a bus station and shoving a tract into the hand of each person who passes by, or sneaking them into mailboxes, or slipping them under the windshield-wipers of automobiles on a parking lot. The most effective witness will be made to those whom we contact day after day at home or at work. This is why each of us — and not merely the preacher — should be an evangelist.

Most readers of this book come in contact with scores of people every week who scarcely know a preacher. But they know you. You work at the same place of employment, under the same boss, and with the same pressures. There's not another person in all the world who is better equipped than you to say, "Christ is my Savior; he died for my sins; he gives me a motive for living, and a hope for the future." If you are too timid to say it with words, hand him a carefully chosen tract, and say, "Here's something that helped me; I hope you'll read it sometime."

Sometimes ordinary conversation gives good opportunities for witness. For example, when folks talk about how quickly time flies — we can remind them that we have just 25,550 *days* at the most, and then we face eternity. But if ordinary conversation does not lead to an opportunity for witness, one can ask several questions. You can say, "By the way, do you have any interest in spiritual things?" And then (regardless of the answer given), say, "Suppose someone were to ask you 'What is a Christian?'—what would you say?" Notice that the question does not pin the person down; it is not saying that he is not a Christian; it is simply an appropriate question that can turn the conversation into channels discussing one's spiritual welfare.

Witnessing is something we learn by doing. Each time we talk about the Christian life, we become more at ease. We learn by experience. We profit from past mistakes. We can build upon strong points gradually discovered.

A tragic note is that vast numbers of church members could not witness to their faith if they wanted to, because they *have* no genuine faith. The methods churches use in receiving new members usually require a minimum of commitment, and many smoothly slip into church membership thinking of the church simply as a nice ethical society that practices a few interesting ordinances, and stands by to offer special services for weddings, illnesses, and funerals. Therefore many of our churches today have become *fields for* evangelism rather than *forces of* evangelism. Each of us needs to examine his own life, and respond to God's call to repentance and cleansing — and then let evangelism become a priority in life.

Sophie, a scrubwoman, used to say that she was called to do two things — to scrub and to preach. Wherever she went, she would tell others about the Savior. Someone made fun of her one day, noting that she was talking about Christ to the wooden Indian standing in front of a cigar store. When she heard the report, she said, "Maybe I did; my eyesight's not too good — but talking about Christ to a wooden Indian isn't nearly as bad as being a wooden Christian who never talks to anybody about him!"

*As a part of the total Christian fellow-
ship the Church of the Brethren has
been entrusted with a message — the
best news of God's love for all persons.
We have also been enlisted in his ministry of reconciliation. But for far too
long we have allowed our uncertainties
to inhibit our evangelism and we have
been hesitant to share enthusiastically
our convictions about God's love and
grace.*

From: *A Statement on Evangelism,*
Annual Conference, 1972

Phyllis Carter, *one of the few women pastors in the Church of the Brethren, has been able to combine her professional responsibilities with duties as a homemaker in a most effective way. Serving the Wabash Church in Indiana, she is also a member of the Ministry Commission of the South/Central Indiana District, and the General Board of her denomination, carrying significant assignments on the Executive Committee, the Goals and Budget Committee, and the World Ministries Commission. Coming from a Quaker background, Phyllis Carter was drawn to the Church of the Brethren through the influence of Dan West and the peace witness of the denomination. Deeply interested in evangelism, she has also shown a concern for causes which relate to social justice and is committed with other pastors in her area to an ecumenical effort to bring a team ministry to her community. She is married and the mother of three children.*

Being an Evangelist

Phyllis Carter

What does it mean to be an evangelist? It is to make God's love known to every person. And the place to share love is where people are. The method is person-to-person, from one heart to another.

For example:

Being an evangelist is Ruby writing a note expressing appreciation for another's personhood and assuring that person of God's love and blessing.

Being an evangelist is Bill bringing alcoholics

and other troubled, hurt, and lonely people to his pastor and the church fellowship, saying, "I just want my friends to know each other."

Being an evangelist is Jack and Nancy stretching their family budget even though they constantly have difficulty in making ends meet, in order to open their home to an unwed mother and her exceptional child for two years.

Being an evangelist is Olden making calls on patients in city hospitals on behalf of another pastor who cannot be there every day.

Being an evangelist is Jim driving across town to pick up children to take them to a church fellowship.

Being an evangelist is Dale listening to the heartaches of a co-worker trapped in an unhappy marriage.

Being an evangelist is John driving to a juvenile center to give support to a teenager who really blew it.

Being an evangelist is Mary going through the obituary column each night so she can write notes of support and sympathy to bereaved families in the name of her church.

Being an evangelist is David serving as a facilitator for concerned persons who are working for prison reform.

Being an evangelist is Bob calling a United States Senator to get action for a young bride whose allotment check has not arrived.

Being an evangelist is Joyce, a young mother, giving herself in friendship to a stranger named Sherrie when Sherrie was working her way back from grief so deep and depression so intense that

she was incapacitated. Joyce thought she was doing nothing special, yet every day while managing
her own household and encouraging a busy young
husband who was building his own business, she
gave time to shopping, sewing, going to church,
listening, being a driver, and giving love that
healed.

Being an evangelist is Sherrie, now a vibrant,
winsome person, giving her friendship and support
to Trish, who faces problems similar to those in
Sherrie's past. When Sherrie questioned Joyce on
the best approach to helping her friend, Joyce's
recommendation was simple, "Listen, really listen.
You don't have to know all the answers, but you
must really care."

BEING AN evangelist is following the example of
all those persons who deliberately take God's love
to a bowling alley, or who in the name of Christ
go to an all-night teenage party as chaperone and
friend, who make calls with police and welfare
workers. who take cookies to a neighbor, who
speak a word of encouragement to a bewildered
politician, who take a prostitute to a township
trustee so she might receive needed financial assistance, who invite a former prison inmate home
for dinner and fellowship with friends, who care
for foster children, and who love the unlovely.

Being an evangelist is holding people's hands
where they are — for God. It is that simple and
that complex. It is a joyful experience; it is utter
pain and frustration; it is seeing some persons
come alive in the knowledge that God is for them,

and it is seeing some persons totally fail. It is knowing that all that matters is obedience to Christ's call to go into all the world and to allow God's love to do all the changing, without condemning or condoning.

Being an evangelist is taking Christ as one's example and recognizing that the strategy for witness centers in love. Jesus brought God's healing love into each situation in a way that produced wholeness among the persons involved. Reading through the gospels, one should look at God's concern for people reflected in the way Christ shows his compassion for persons like us — for the poor, the disinherited, for women, for the common people, and for all who suffer discrimination because of custom, family, or religion.

Being an evangelist is expressing love for people around you — the attendant at the service station, the receptionist at the hospital desk, the waitress, the bank teller, the mailman, the bus or taxi driver — to name only a few. It means recognizing that God wants to heal and to bring hope, to see lives fulfilled, and to bring renewal out of despair.

Being an evangelist means valuing each person as a human being, really being with that person, and taking him seriously as he is. When people focus their interest deeply into another's life, something happens between them. Divine love shines into people's hearts through the beam of our concern. This deep concern for a person in the present moment is the greatest kind of love we can give. When a person undergoes the inner experience of abandonment to God's love and obedience to his summons, then he knows God's love and seeks in every way to make that love known to all persons. Sometimes we make it all too hard. We dig too deep, philosophize, and theologize too much.

WE NEED to break loose from our mediocrity and to believe God for everything he has. Our confidence is not in ourselves but in Christ. As we experience his love, we must speak of what we have seen and heard. One does not need to be an important churchman to do big things for God. One can still learn to love people on their terms, and to act as a channel for God's love.

This person-to-person sharing of the best news is urgent. There are sermons that need to be preached in the lives of those who believe in Jesus Christ. No special oratory is required, nor is there need for notes or manuscript. The message comes from one heart to another's heart. We need to see every human encounter, every event and experience, as already filled with God's presence. That presence may be felt in moments of tender love, in a time of forgiveness and reconciliation. The place to share love is where people are, at fun and play, in the apartment project, in the glitter and glamor of horse or dog shows, and in the ghettos and gutters. Every situation counts. For every person is a child of promise whether or not he knows it, likes it, or wants it.

The members of the body of Christ have too long sat in their comfortable pews, talking about the need for some program or strategy of evangelism and looking for someone to minister to that need. We Christians seem to involve ourselves endlessly in a careful study of the wrong questions. We are always looking for some new project or some new program that makes us relevant. But when we are looking for our own relevant image, we are seldom interested in people and movements for their own sake and fulfillment.

ONE OF the greatest challenges for our generation is to find the proper balance between institutionalized discipleship and personal discipleship. Jesus sought out the needy. That is what we must do. We must escape the pigeonhole of the pew to discover anew the personal aspect of the gospel. This does not mean that meeting together is unimportant. For Christians need to speak God's word to one another. No person can be a Christian alone. We are one in Christ. The spirit of God is not promised to the individual alone. Rather, it is promised to the fellowship of Christian brothers and sisters. It is in our gathering together, in our seeking to *become*, that we become free as a body and as individuals. We stimulate each other to know God and our other persons. Our unity comes as we serve.

One recent writer has stated, "There is no Christian community not rooted in service, and no Christian service not rooted in relationship." It is out of this sense of being a called people that the whole church, whether a local congregation, or individual members of the body, can move out to be evangelists. We will not be able to answer every need in the world around us, nor are we intended to. But because of the discovery of who we are and in the very act of stirring gifts within each other we receive guidance. We will know what our specific mission is. At some points our evangelistic task will be fulfilled through the channels of ecumenical efforts.

To be an evangelist is to respond to the call of God whether that call comes individually, through a local congregation or from the entire Brotherhood. To respond does not require that we withdraw from areas of social or political responsibility but rather that we perceive God's presence and action in the whole range of human activities. We dare not neglect the gathering together for worship and nurture by which the church receives strength for its scattering — in witness and service. But the scattering is also important in helping us be evangelists. For we cannot be true disciples of Jesus without becoming personally involved in the suffering and need of humanity.

DeWitt L. Miller *has been minister of the Church of the Brethren in Hagerstown, Maryland, since 1954, where his ministry has not been limited to members of his congregation but has included significant community service to such agencies as Good-will Industries and the YMCA. His strong ecumenical commitment has provided leadership in many interdenominational enterprises such as Key '73, for which he was chairman for the churches in his county. DeWitt Miller was moderator of Annual Conference in 1964. He has participated in the British-American Pulpit Exchange and in the exchange visits between the Church of the Brethren and the Russian Orthodox Church. With Mrs. Miller, he also directed an International Peace Seminar in Germany. His books include* You and Your Church, *at one time a popular study guide on the meaning of church membership.*

5

Let's Go Fishing

DeWitt L. Miller

The most exciting thing I know about the Church of the Brethren right now is the way it is discovering the important place that evangelism should have in the life of the church.

Evangelism has not been exactly "our thing" as Brethren. We have rationalized this in many ways. Some with a phony sort of modesty have said that religious experience is such a personal thing that you cannot talk with just anybody about it. But we can talk with almost anybody about everything else that is meaningful to us: politics and taxes, food and sports, the latest neighborhood gossip, the work in which we are engaged, and our latest purchase whether it be a home, a car, a new bit of clothing, a new power lawn mower, or an air conditioner; but we think we could never talk to persons about God and their relationship to him. Nonsense!

I know a minister who proposed that his church try to get 100 new members from among the unchurched people of the community. He was told, "We aren't interested in numbers." But do not those numbers represent people-persons who are children of God, in whose *present good* and eternal destiny we should be interested? He was told that people today are interested in religion but not in the church, and that this evangelism bit is just for the purpose of building an organization and institution. But that has as much sense to it as for a fellow to tell a girl he loves her, but he never takes her hand, never looks into her eyes, never takes her into his arms, never kisses her, never gives her a gift. The spirit has always had to have a body, and when God wanted to reveal himself to his people he took the body of a man. Religion has to have a body, and that body is the church.

We Brethren have had our own special escape hatch. We would rather feed hungry people, give refugees a home, and demonstrate against war. We like to get religion down where you can milk it, as the mass media said of the heifer program. How proud we were. And that in itself is not bad. If we ever quit doing things like that we will lose the right to be called Brethren. The Good Samaritan and the Golden Rule are as much a part of the gospel as doctrine and theology. Proclaiming the message of the good life for all people and working for it diligently and sacrificially in down-to-earth ways has been our bag, and in the plan of God this may be our greatest contribution to the church of Jesus Christ.

But unless this traditional emphasis is rooted in an experience of being born again, our very genius can become a humanistic do-goodism and a holier-than-thou corporate selfishness. I nearly gagged when a young person came home from a youth conference and told me she had discovered that it is more important to be Brethren than to be Christian. Whenever you and I feel that we can be Brethren without first of all knowing ourselves as children of God, we are really mixed up religiously. It is high time that Brethren and all other Christians learn about the evangel, the good news of God's love, the good news that God was in Christ reconciling the world unto himself. To proclaim the good news we need to be evangelists, and to get the job done the church needs a program of evangelism.

However, not everything that has been called evangelism has been true to the New Testament description of evangelism. I have read many definitions of both the word and the idea, and one of my favorites comes from D. T. Niles, who says: "Evangelism is one beggar telling another beggar where to find bread." It is hard to improve on that one, and you can think and pray about it for a long time before all its meaning will be exhausted. It gives the lie to the idea that the evangelist is better than the one being evangelized, that you have to be a saint to introduce other persons to God. It simply means that you know One who forgives your sin, who takes away the burden of your guilt, who releases you into the freedom of the new life in Christ Jesus, and that what he has done for you he can do for others. It simply says that because God loves you, you want all persons to know that he loves them too.

In spite of the beauty and wonder of that definition from one of the great spirits of the third world, I would like to suggest for our consideration a different definition. Evangelism is like a two-sided coin. The first side is *God calling you and me to put first in our lives the doing of God's will and helping him to help other people in their need.*

The other side of the coin is that *evangelism is an enlistment in which God uses us as his enlistment officers to get others to enlist in this work too.* Now the truth is that you cannot have one without the other if you are a follower of Jesus. If we are not doing the second it is probably because the first has not really happened to us, but if we have responded to God's call we are very likely already doing the second for the two go together like ham and eggs, bread and butter, salt and pepper, boy and girl.

There is no place to see how this works out any better than in a story related in Matthew's gospel. Jesus was walking by the Sea of Galilee and he saw five young men and an older man, the father of one of them, mending their nets. Apparently they had just returned from a fishing trip and were getting the nets in shape so they could go back out for another try at fishing. And Jesus said to them, "Follow me, and I will make you fishers of men." He did not say, "Follow me, and I will make you better persons." He did not say, "Follow me, and I will make you successful." He did not say, "Follow me, and I will make you more attractive, dynamic persons."

Jesus did not say, "Follow me, and I will make you rich." He did not say, "Follow me, and I will make you over so that you can make friends and influence people." He did not say, "Follow me, and I will make life easier for you." In fact, later he told them that the only pathway of discipleship was the *via dolorosa,* the way of the cross — the way of cross bearing. We do not come to Christ for what we get out of it. That would be selfish and that is sin. We follow him in service and in love.

Jesus did, however, say on another occasion, that if you seek first the kingdom of right relations all these other things which men selfishly desire will be yours as well. Now this is not double-talk on the part of Jesus. He is simply saying that our motivation must be right. We are to live for God and to help people. This is our purpose; this is our aim — the direction of our lives. In the long stretch of time and eternity as we become more and more like Jesus we will achieve the kind of success which is the concern of the kingdom of God; we will become more charming and attractive to people because of our genuine love for others and our interest and caring for them; we will possess and enjoy the necessary material things, if not the luxuries for which men selfishly aspire. We will have the opportunity to help change our world so that God's will might be done on earth as it is in heaven, and we will be more and more rid of the self-defeating pressures and demands that prostitue and deplete our resources of body, mind, and spirit.

So when Jesus said, "Follow me," he was saying, "Follow me in loving concern for those all around you who are working themselves into ulcers and nervous breakdowns trying to possess things and manipulate people." He is still saying, "Follow me in sympathy and understanding. Follow me by taking time to help persons. Follow me in giving yourselves to each other in love."

Many years ago in Cleveland a young teenager fell under the influence and into the clutches of an older and unscrupulous woman. All his parental training and all the influence of his home were unable to keep him from getting in trouble with the law. After his conviction by the court, because of his youth, the sentence was suspended and he was released into the custody of his parents. But he could not face his friends at his church. When the family came to church the boy stayed at home; but each Sunday when the others came home he would take his younger brother off in the corner and ask, "Did anybody ask about me?"

Here was a desperate, pathetic soul crying out, "Does anybody care?"

How many people who live within the shadow of your house wonder if you care? And what have you done recently to let anyone know that you care? Jesus said, "Follow me and I will make you fishers of men. I will send you out into the highways and byways of your town and countryside to bring in the persons who need help." These men to whom Jesus was speaking caught fish for a living; they were soon to catch men for God. No matter what you do for a living, God wants you to catch men for him. And what better help can you bring to others than to introduce them to Jesus Christ, to get them to commit their lives to him and to his way of unselfish service, to get their minds off their own self-centeredness and on to God and his redemptive and reconciling purposes?

The only way to be saved is to save somebody else. Not that we do the saving — only God can do that — but we must bring people to God, introduce them to Jesus Christ, and encourage them to accept him as Lord and Master, joining with us in obedience to the things he commanded, following the rule of love, entering into right relationships with others and ministering to human need in God's name. Then they too will discover "salvation" as they become fishers of men!

John's Gospel tells us that as soon as Andrew met Jesus, he ran to get his brother Peter. What more Christian response is there to finding God, to learning to know Jesus Christ? Go get your brothers. Peter and Andrew, along with James and John, left their nets, a symbol of all self-centered, self-serving activity and followed Jesus that he might make them fishers of men. But they also left their father. Have you ever looked closely at Hoffman's painting, *The Call of the Fishermen?* The faces of the young men are eager and filled with a fascination for Jesus, but the face of the father is the face of tradition, the face of business, the face of practicality, the face of "no-risk," the face of the establishment. The father seems to be saying, "I don't yet see it, besides, if I don't look after me, who will? If I don't make the business succeed by any means necessary, we will be in deep trouble."

But the boys were different. You see in their face the risk of high adventure, the pursuit of far-off goals. There is a response there to an appeal to use their talents in exciting ways that have to do with the most precious commodity this world knows anything about — people. Peter, Andrew, James, and John were fishermen with no formal education — the only education they ever had was to be with Jesus for three years — and they had their weaknesses. Peter was profane and swore as only some hard hats know how to swear. James and John had such uncontrollable tempers they were called "sons of thunder." If Jesus wanted them, he surely wants you. If Jesus could use them, he could certainly use you. If Jesus could use them, he could certainly use you. If they could become his evangelists, you can too.

By the time the day of Pentecost had come there were 120 who had responded to the call of Jesus. They went out from the Upper Room to win — to enlist — 3000 the first day and more every day thereafter until, as the historian said, they had turned the world upside down and shaken the Roman Empire to its foundations. If they could do that, think what the church today can do, especially if every adult, every mother and father, every young person, every boy and girl will agree to serve God in the evangelistic program of the church.

When we look at our own land and across our world today there seems to me more truth than ever in the words of Jesus, "Behold! The fields are white unto the harvest but the laborers are too few." It is time for us to take each other by the hand right now and say, "Let's go fishing!"

Thomas Wilson *has been a member of the staff of the General Board of the Church of the Brethren since 1969, serving as consultant for church and community involvement for the Parish Ministries Commission. Following his graduation from Bethany Theological Seminary, he was employed for one year by the Cook County Department of Public Aid. He then served for eight years as pastor of First Church of the Brethren in Chicago during which time he helped his interracial congregation to adapt their program to the needs of a changing neighborhood. While now living with his wife and three children in Elgin, Illinois, he has continued his involvement in Chicago's inner city through his membership on the Board of Trustees of Bethany Brethren-Garfield Park Community Hospital. He has been a member of the General Board of his denomination and serves his church as a representative on several commissions of the National Council of Churches.*

Everyday Witnessing to Everyday People

6

Thomas Wilson

Sly and the Family Stone, a popular rock group, feature a song about "everyday people" whose beliefs are in their song. Our concern in this chapter is with "everyday Christians" and their calling to witness to everyday people.

The world is the context within which everyday people exist — everyday. It is also the arena within which Christians are called to live out their lives and bear everyday witness to the Savior of the world and Lord of history. There are many kinds of Christians, but an everyday Christian is one who, though he is thoroughly immersed in the world, is being saved from the world and is therefore free to minister to it.

The gospel itself calls us to be everyday Christians. Jesus said, "If anyone comes after me he must deny himself, take up his cross, and follow me daily." His command to us is the same as that which he gave to the early church, "Go therefore and make disciples of all the nations, baptizing them in the name of the Father, and the Son, and the Holy Spirit, teaching them to observe all things I have commanded you." Much has been made of the word *go* in this command. A close reading of the text in the language of the early church reveals that it is not an imperative as we read it in English so much as a participle that may be translated rather literally like this, "As you go, disciple all nations."

This suggests that Jesus took it for granted that his followers would be involved in the life of the world, that they would be going into every nation in the course of their everyday affairs. Also he proposed that evangelism should be the calling of all Christians, that as they went about their everyday business (their vocations) they would find time to spread the gospel and to make disciples.

This insight is not new, but it has revolutionary implications: (1) that the church can somehow divest itself of its Sunday mentality, and (2) that it can develop a strategy of penetration whereby it can truly become leaven, light, and salt in all the structures of society.

THERE is a high privilege in the responsibility inherent in the call of Christians to daily discipleship. We are all parts of Christ's body with functions to perform that are crucial for the development of his church. Recently within the church there has come a new emmergence and emphasis upon the ministry of the laity, and lay persons are rising to this challenge. As a matter of fact, there are many advantages that the lay minister has over the professional minister, as Elton Trueblood has pointed out in his book, *Your Other Vocation*.

First of all, it is easier for the everyday Christian to know persons as they are, since many people tend to put on masks in the presence of the professional minister. During my seminary training in Chicago, I was employed one summer vacation at a large factory. For two months I purposely failed to disclose to my co-workers that I was studying and preparing for the ministry. They knew I was a student, but they did not know I was a theological student.

I came to know persons in a relationship of work. I learned something about their language, their mode of thought, their joys and sorrows, and their hopes and aspirations. I even learned to live with their profanity. It was not until the beginning of the third and final month of summer vacation that I told several of them that I was preparing for the Christian ministry. The word spread rapidly. It was amazing how many of them came to me apologizing for things they had said and done in my presence. It became apparent that because I functioned in this situation as a lay person it was much easier for me than for a minister to know such persons as they really are.

Also, many persons have tuned out the professional minister and are no longer listening to what he has to say simply because they think he is expected to say certain things. For this reason the everyday lay Christian is free from any stigma of professionalism. What he says is often taken more seriously than what the minister says. Family visitation also may be more effective when undertaken by a lay person. His call is accepted as an evidence of genuine conviction, of concern and friendship, whereas some families may think the minister is only doing what is expected of him.

The everyday Christian is close to life as it is experienced by other lay persons. He is already working in the midst of everyday life. During another summer when I was earning some extra money as a cab driver in Chicago I recall late one evening when a sophisticated lady flagged my cab on Chicago near Michigan Avenue. When I asked "Where to?" she replied, "North on the lake." She immediately began talking, very rationally, about herself and the world. I soon realized that this lady, however, was deeply troubled. After driving north for quite a ways I also discovered she had no particular destination. She rode for quite awhile, running up a considerable fee on the meter, but she continued to talk and talk and talk. I do not remember the details of the conversation, but what stands out vividly in my memory is that this person had a need and wanted someone to listen to her. I happened to be there at the point of need.

Everyday Christians can bring to the task of witnessing a certain freshness, an openness to new ways of thinking and doing that may not be evident to the professional minister. We ought never to belittle individual witness. On the other hand, we must recognize the validity of the corporate witness. Our coming together constitutes a witness in itself.

Perhaps I can best illustrate some of the ways in which everyday Christians witness to everyday people by describing in some detail the ministry of an integrated church in the westside slums of Chicago, sometimes referred to euphemistically as the inner city.

As the pastor of the First Church of the Brethren in Chicago I sometimes greeted parishioners on the outside steps of the church following morning worship. The street in front of the church was a main thoroughfare and bus route. Often there were people in apartment windows and others sitting or walking on the sidewalks near the church. Many times people came to me, people who had observed the friendly dialogue or the frequent embracing of blacks and whites outside the church, with the question: "What kind of a church is this?" When an individual or a congregation by word and deed prompts questions such as this, a vast arena is opened with a potential for unlimited evangelizing.

Our congregation had all of the conventional program opportunities — women's circle, boy scouts, girl scouts, worship and preaching services, church school classes for all ages, prayer and Bible study, counselling, undershepherd groups, visitation program, elective study groups, adult, youth, and children's choirs. But still, as the church began to respond to the needs that were peculiar and unique for persons living under the conditions existing in that community, a completely new list of programs emerged.

The world, in this case the East Garfield Community, had powerfully laid on the church's doorstep its agenda. Our congregation concluded that it could not be the church of Jesus Christ in this situation and ignore the human needs that were crying out for answers and solutions, human needs that were both material and spiritual. So this church became allied with some national groups and with other religious communions, Catholic and Protestant, and secular organizations and agencies in this community, to bring to that community many needed changes. Our goal was to proclaim Christ as Savior and Lord and bring all the structures of society, whether they were social, economical, or political, under the judgment of God, even as we stood under the judgment.

In a densely populated community where virtually no new housing had been built in fifty years, in which the existing housing had already been used by seven or eight national, ethnic or racial groups, where the vacancy rate was less than one percent and with slumlords gouging the poor, we hired a community organizer who became instrumental in organizing a rent strike against the largest slumholder in the community, the owner or manager of more than forty multiple-dwelling properties. This action culminated in the signing of a contractual agreement and a declaration of the rights of both landlords and tenants, in 1968 in the church's basement. The signing of this document before more than sixty representatives of the news media was hailed as a first in the country. To some extent it eased the way for legal recognition of tenant rights and opened doors for dealing with the broader problem of providing open housing in an open society.

During two boycotts of the public school system, Freedom Schools were operated in the basement of the church to accentuate the need for changes in the educational system that would bring quality education to all children.

The church attempted to improve the economic conditions of the area also. While newspaper headlines boasted that Chicago was the richest city in the world and that unemployment was less than five percent, persistent unemployment of eligible males in some areas of our community reached thirty-five percent, with underemployment being equally a problem. One third of the population was receiving some kind of public assistance. Lending institutions that provided blacks with money to purchase new appliances, color television sets, and new automobiles, refused to provide money for home improvements for the same persons. In various ways we attempted to provide direct and referral services to meet the needs and expose the problems.

THE CHURCH also attempted to minister in the area of government and politics. A change in the color complexion of this neighborhood resulted in noticeable changes in services provided to the residents. Garbage collection was cut back from twice to once a week. The frequency of street cleaning decreased, while the number of policemen increased. Instead of servants and protectors, the latter were looked upon as an occupying force who frequently harassed and deprived residents of their basic legal rights. They were also understood to be an arm of the powerful political machine, providing ears, eyes, and muscles for continuing its control while depriving the residents of decision-making powers relative to their own political destiny.

The congregation, individually and collectively, entered the political arena by sponsoring candidates, working within the structures to establish better police-community relationships and services to the community, and to liberate those who were oppressed.

In the area of health care we had the technical knowhow but lacked a system of delivery. North Lawndale, a community near us, had the highest infant mortality rate (one death out of every four births) in the United States and higher than any country in the Western Hemisphere. This was true in spite of the fact that the community was in the shadow of one of the greatest health complexes in the world. This too provided a part of our agenda.

Other programs included a food pantry and material aid, various club programs for children and teens, a special ministry to approximately ten interracial couples, and a ministry to senior citizens in a nearby apartment complex.

When violence erupted in cities across the country in 1968, following the death of Martin Luther King, Jr., Chicago did not escape, nor did the community in which we ministered. What is more memorable than the violence was a small group of Christians, black and white, who, on the Sunday following King's death, literally walked past soldiers occupying the steps of the church in an air heavy with the stench of smoke and gunfire — heavy too with hate and hostility. They filed into church to wash each other's feet, even as they had attempted to wash the feet of the world, and to participate in the love feast and communion service. As they broke bread, fellowshiped, and drank together, washing each other's feet and embracing, they knew in that moment, so pregnant with meaning, they had been saved from bigotry, the sin of judging others by skin color or by status in life, and were called to a life of love, of giving and forgiving, and to witnessing and embodying that love in such a time as this.

These experiences as everyday Christians validated for us the good news of Jesus Christ and the real meaning of evangelism. Several things came through with clarity as we endeavored to witness to what God had done and was doing in our lives. We made some glorious discoveries:

Good news is a person! It is not just an announcement of God's love. It is God in Jesus Christ redeeming the world (John 3:16). It is the Christlike spirit embodying itself in the life of a people whose task is to be bearers of the good news. Embodiment is the essential means of communicating the good news among persons. For many people living in our community we were the only Christ they would ever see or experience.

Good news is practical! God's message to persons in the world is not theoretical or abstract. The evidence of his love is ultimately demonstrated in the birth of Jesus and the giving of God's only son to die for the world. Good news requires this kind of flesh and blood involvement and identification of God with persons. This is the meaning of Emmanuel — God with us. God works through persons to show his love in specific, concrete, and practical ways.

Good news is a servant! The life-style of the bearers of good news is characterized by the servant motif. Our technology and ingenuity make this an extremely difficult lesson to learn in the twentieth century. Our movements tend to lead us away from the servant role. John the Baptist, who was ill-clothed, unshaven, and smelling of foul odors, would be unwelcome in the clean, carpeted, and cushioned surroundings of most contemporary Christians. There is a striking similarity between John and modern day prophets who bring judgment upon contemporary life.

Everyday Christians who speak out against military escalation, political, racial, and economic injustices, inequities in job opportunities, poor housing, and inadequate schools stand more in the mainstream of God's historic purpose for mankind than those who isolate themselves from the care and concern of others and who are content to insist that one's religious experience must be a private affair. Everyday Christians should affirm the vertical relationship of persons with God, but they ought never to neglect the horizontal relationship with their neighbors.

Good news is liberation! Jesus declared the purpose of his coming was to preach release to the captives and the setting free of those who were oppressed. Good news is the freeing of persons from individual guilt, fears, and anxieties. It is freeing persons from all systems that oppress.

Good news is powerful! Most places visited by the apostles were never the same after they had been there. Their presence provided a channel through which a transforming power was at work (Acts 14:10).

Finally, the good news is a challenge! It challenges persons to be changed at the very core of their being. It challenges the way one thinks and sees and what one does. It calls for a commitment of one's life to Christ and his way of life.

Evangelism is telling the good news, being the good news, and doing the good news. It calls forth a responsive commitment to that good news and to the new life and new community that God is bringing into being.

In this new community everyday Christians engage themselves in the lives of everyday people. They are keenly aware of what Finley B. Edge states in *The Greening of the Church,* that "what ultimately happens in the world depends upon what first happens in the local church." They possess the unique capacity to live and witness with relevance to everyday people in an everyday world.

Merlin E. Garber *has served three parishes, in Champaign, Illinois; Roanoke, Virginia; and Frederick, Maryland, where he presently ministers. Under his leadership, the Frederick Church of the Brethren has become one of the largest in the Brotherhood. His deep commitment to evangelism has not only helped to develop a strong evangelical emphasis in his own congregation, but has given him opportunity for leadership in many workshops on effective congregational witness. Merlin Garber and his wife have traveled extensively. They served for two years as directors of a Brethren Service project in Austria. Their special interests have been in the field of pre-Columbian civilization and Mayan culture as well as biblical geography. The Garbers are the parents of two children and several foster children.*

Accept the Mandate, Receive the Power, and Go

7

Merlin E. Garber

If you want to be evangelistic consider Pentecost. Here was evangelism at its very best. Here was involvement. Here was power. Here was success. No other single incident in church history has matched it for sheer enthusiasm and excitement. It is the belief of many, if not most, Christians that whoever attempts to be evangelistic must not only be familiar with, but also experience, a personal Pentecost. What did happen at Pentecost? What was it that set in motion the movement that was to upset the world? A careful analysis will indicate that at least three elements were involved.

The first was the mandate. This we have called the Great Commission. The very last thing Jesus said to his disciples was, "Go ye therefore, and teach all nations, baptizing them in the name of the Father, and of the Son, and of the Holy Spirit; teaching them to observe all things whatsoever I have commanded you; and lo, I am with you always, even unto the end of the world. Amen!" (Matthew 28:19-20).

The mandate seems simple enough. Yet there has been much confusion and misunderstanding regarding it. Many have considered it extra-curricular, an elective which one can select if one desires. Therefore it has not held top priority. Its primary importance must be recognized if the church is to be evangelistic.

However, the problem does not end there. Many people believe in the primacy of the mandate, but they say, "Primacy for whom?" They believe that it is the specialized work of a few — such persons as the minister, the professional evangelist, or some select group of specially gifted people.

Recently in a workshop I was trying to make the point that evangelism is for everybody when a critic took issue with the statement. He contended that the commission was given to just the apostles and not to other Christians. He regarded the mandate as intended for a select few but not for him. It is my belief that only when we realize that evangelism is for everybody will we have any measure of success. Whatever success I have encountered in my ministry has been the result of lay persons accepting this commission as theirs.

Another important aspect of the mandate is that it was meant to be not only the most important task but the lifework of every person. This does not mean that we do not have other occupations. Paul was a tentmaker. We may be teachers, lawyers, farmers, students, doctors, or whatever vocation we choose; but while we may support ourselves by these occupations, our life's work is to win men to Christ. Once a person begins to understand this, his life takes on a new dimension and a new direction. There seems to be little doubt that the first generation of Christians understood this. There was no arguing the point for them. They believed in the Great Commission. They believed it was top priority. They believed it was for everyone who named the name of Christ. They believed it was their life's work.

THE SECOND element at Pentecost was commitment. It is very easy to give lip service to the Great Commission. Many people believe in it. They just don't do it. A well-known leader tells of being invited to conduct an evangelism workshop. When he got there he found a large number of apparently interested people. They wanted to know all about evangelism. So he spent about three days giving the scriptural background and explaining the techniques. Then he announced that the remaining time would be spent in fieldwork putting into practice the things they had learned. To this the group replied with dismay, "You don't understand. We just wanted to make a study of it. We didn't want to *do* it!"

Unfortunately that seems to be the prevailing attitude of many church people today. We want to learn about evangelism. We don't want to practice it.

Perhaps the least understood part of the total Pentecostal experience is what has been called by some the "tarry time." After Jesus had given his mandate he went on to say that the disciples should *tarry* for awhile. What was the purpose of this period? I am firmly convinced it was the time given the disciples to make up their minds. Some believe that this was a prayer time during which the disciples were to pray for the coming of the Holy Spirit. This does not seem to be the case. It is true that they prayed, but there is no evidence that they prayed for the coming of the Spirit. In fact, this would have been an affront to the Lord who had already promised that the Spirit would be forthcoming. What they prayed for was that they might be committed to carrying out the mandate.

This was no easy decision. A commitment to the mandate would make significant changes in their lives. It involved a discussion of the nature of the work to which they were being called, changes in their plans, reflections about the locations in which the work would take place. One cannot make such a commitment without considering all of these. Such a decision required real soul-searching. It necessitated a refining and defining of their personal relationship with the Lord.

They must have agonized over the decision. They prayed fervently.

Perhaps the major question they had to wrestle with was what would happen to the group if they made such a commitment. The pressure to form a commune, to live in secure isolation from the hostile world was undoubtedly there. To accept the Great Commission would destroy such protective community. Some sociologists are convinced that perhaps the greatest decision made by the early church was their decision *not* to stay together. Jesus had said, "Go into all the world." Their response was evident in the simple statement, "They went everywhere."

One other thing happened in the Upper Room during their tarry time that fits into the evangelistic mosaic. They voted for another apostle to take the place of Judas. In other words they wanted to be at full force when they embarked on their mission.

The Scriptures speak of the one hundred and twenty being of one accord. That is, they all had become committed. Evangelism is dependent upon a conscious, voluntary commitment of the individual and/or the group to carry out literally and fully the great commission. Elton Trueblood in his book *The Company of the Committed* contends that only those who are committed to witnessing are really in the church. Are *you* in the church? Is the group to which you belong really a church? If our thesis is correct, the church was born at the time the commitment was made.

The third element was power. Jesus gave his mandate. He told his followers to wait until they were committed. Then they were to receive power. What was that power and what was it to be used for? Any reading would seem to lead one to the obvious conclusion that the power was to carry out the mandate. It was the power to witness. However, this needs some interpretation. It was indeed the power to witness but it was not only that. It was something more. And it is this "something more" that makes the difference. The real power, which the disciples understood, was not just the power to witness but to be *effective* in witnessing.

Many people can witness but they are not effective. Sometimes they drive people away instead of drawing them to the Lord. The power that came upon the group of committed disciples was the power to move men Godward. No less an authority than charismatic Charles Finney asserts that the Pentecostal power was the power to fasten "saving impressions" upon men and women. He further asserts that this was undoubtedly what the disciples understood Christ to promise. When the power came upon them it was so strong that not even language was a barrier. They began to speak to the assembled throng, and three thousand persons were converted that very hour. When this power comes upon us, we too move men to God.

I have talked with a number of people who have been charged with this power. They state that it often manifests itself in a surprising manner. Sometimes a single sentence, a word, a gesture, a touch of the hand, or even a look will convey this power in an overcoming manner. God, speaking in and through them, makes a saving impression. I have observed this in others, and there have been seasons when I too have experienced it. When this happens, people are converted.

Let us assume for the moment we are in agreement that these elements are necessary and that we accept them. The question then arises as to how we can vitalize them. We must act upon them and let them act upon us. Each one requires a specialized acceptance or action for it to become productive. I would caution anyone not to begin his fieldwork until such time as he has, for instance, reordered his priorities and given Christ's commission its rightful place. This may take time. It did at Pentecost.

When the commitment has been made, then one must open one's life to the Spirit. However, the Spirit works according to his own direction and not by any preconceived plan we may have. But the Spirit has been promised and Christ will not go back upon his Word. In fact, he is already within us waiting to be appropriated. All we need to do, as Paul stated to Timothy, is to stir up the gift of God within us. Lest anyone misunderstand these comments and feel that evangelism is really something *we* do, let me hasten to say it is really something that *God* does through us. Every human resource must be actively placed at God's disposal.

So FAR we have talked about the nature of evangelism. We have not discussed technique. There is a technique to be used. It may vary with different individuals, but my experience indicates that some given technique is necessary. The following is the one I use and that many successful soul winners follow.

First of all, select a prospect, a specific person or several persons, not people in general. The prospect may be someone very close to you, or a casual friend, or even a complete stranger. However, it must be someone for whom you have a burning concern. This person then is placed on your prayer list and daily lifted to God for his intercession. My experience has been that very few persons are really won to the Lord for whom earnest prayer has not been made.

The next step is intentionally to make some contact. A study of New Testament evangelism indicates that it was aggressive. I mean that evangelists were eager that something happen. Either they arranged circumstances or took advantage of the circumstances which God arranged. However, in either case they were active. The Junior Chamber of Commerce used to have a slogan, "Nothing just happens." Certainly in evangelism nothing just happens. It is made to happen.

But you must earn the right to speak. Many people are driven away because of premature overtures. When to speak is a matter of the Spirit's direction. When the fullness of time has arrived, you then give your witness. Precisely what to speak is impossible to say. There is no stereotyped message and if our witness becomes so it loses its effectiveness. We naturally and informally share the good news that in Christ we have God's offer of new life. We give our testimony to what this has meant in our own lives — the forgiveness of our sins, restored fellowship, a personal relationship with the Lord Jesus that acknowledges him as Savior and Lord, and a confidence in the fulfillment of all of God's promises.

The final step is to ask for a decision. Specifically ask the person to accept Christ. Precisely at this point most evangelism breaks down. Either the person rushes in where angels fear to tread and blows the whole thing by premature and ill-considered soliciting, or he fails to ask the important question at all. Of the two courses of action, it seems that we fail most with the latter. Rufus Bucher used to say that we try to be so tactful that we never make any contact at all.

In my earlier ministry I tried hard to win people to the Lord. It seemed that they were attracted to my preaching. They seemed to like me as a person. They believed in the doctrines, but they joined other churches. I was at a loss to account for this. Much later I discovered why. The other ministers were asking the people to join their churches. I was all the time hinting, suggesting, implying, but never really asking for a decision. This seems to be the common weakness of most would-be soul winners. We never get to the real issue. I find that evangelism is like courtship. One is attracted to another individual. He arranges circumstances so as to meet and be with the other person. He then woos. When he has wooed and won, he pops the question. I believe that people must be literally loved into the kingdom. There is no mechanical procedure that will serve as a substitute.

I would like to conclude with an invitation. Accept the mandate of Christ. Commit yourself to carrying it out. Receive the promised power and go forth in the Lord's name. The time is urgent. The fields are white unto the harvest. Remember, above all else, you are not called upon to defend the gospel but to proclaim it. You are not even called to be successful but to be faithful. If, however, as a result of your efforts someone is saved, let it be known "that he which converted a sinner from the error of his way shall save a soul from death and shall hide a multitude of sins."

Surely we are called to be more positive in affirming our loyalty to Jesus Christ and more aggressive in seeking commitments to him, to his church, and to his kingdom. As persons, as congregations, as a Brotherhood, we prayerfully anticipate the renewal of faith that will be reflected in a desire to grow, to be fruitful and multiply — both for the glory of God and for our neighbor's good.

From: *A Statement on Evangelism,*
Annual Conference, 1972

R. Russell Bixler *came to the pastoral ministry after seven years in business. He was for thirteen years minister of the Church of the Brethren in Pittsburgh, Pennsylvania, the church to which he went directly upon completion of his seminary education. He is currently an associate pastor of that church, being relieved of most of his pastoral functions so that he can devote more time to charismatic renewal. He is president and chairman of the board of the Western Pennsylvania Christian Broadcasting Company which is seeking to establish a Christian television station in the area. He is also chairman of the planning committee for the annual Greater Pittsburgh Charismatic Conference, involving thousands of participants, and has become increasingly involved in a growing ministry of preaching and teaching in the charismatic movement. He is married and the father of four children. His popular book,* It Can Happen to Anybody, *is now in its sixth printing.*

8

Give the
Hard Work
to the Holy Spirit

R. Russell Bixler

Chuck had been an alcoholic since World War II. Each year his problem had grown worse. He was drinking a fifth of whiskey every day. Chuck grew up a "nominal" Lutheran, but because of his embarrassment he had not attended his church in a long time.

Some friends — Bill and Betty — suggested to Chuck that he go to church with them one Sunday evening. "It's *different*," persuaded Bill, himself a loyal Presbyterian. Chuck reluctantly agreed to attend the service at the Pittsburgh Church of the Brethren.

That evening Chuck sat rather uncomfortably for a period, gradually warming to the joyous singing. Then he heard testimones of how Jesus Christ had worked miracles in various lives. Chuck felt strangely different when he left. No one had touched him; no one spoke to him about his "problem." But when he returned home Chuck went to bed without a drink for the first time in twenty-five years.

This incident — with varying details — is duplicated each week in the Pittsburgh Church of the Brethren. It is the continuing fulfillment of Jesus' promise: "But you shall receive power when the Holy Spirit has come upon you; and you shall be my witnesses" (Acts 1:8).

Chuck was free! He was so grateful to Jesus Christ that he committed his life to him. Suddenly Chuck *knew* that Jesus loved him — loved him in spite of the mess he was. His sins were forgiven! God had given him eternal life! Chuck was born again, a new creation in Christ. Immediately he noticed, to his surprise, a burning desire to read the Bible.

Chuck asked about joining our congregation. He was offended at my response: "Go back to your own church and glow!"

Reluctantly at first but now enthusiastically, Chuck has been "glowing" as a lay leader in his own congregation — with some rather happy results.

God HAS turned my theology upside down repeatedly in the last few years. And I was a pastor who thought he knew his Bible! We become so accustomed to traditional or cultural methods of evangelism that the *biblical* methods are often obscured from our understanding. When Jesus told a leper, "The Father loves you," he didn't merely *say* those words — he fulfilled them! Jesus reached out his hand and touched the leper: "Be clean!" And the leprosy disappeared.

There is normally a response of commitment on the part of one who receives such love, although that love is not offered with any strings attached. The person so blessed wants to follow — to belong to — Jesus. "We love, because he first loved us" (1 John 4:19). Until an individual first experiences that divine love of God, he has nothing to respond *to*. The touch of Jesus Christ is quite personal, individually tailored. "And a vast crowd brought him their lame, blind, maimed, and those who couldn't speak, and many others, and laid them before Jesus, and he healed them all. What a spectacle it was! Those who had not been able to say a word before were talking excitedly, and those with missing arms and legs had new ones; the crippled were walking and jumping around, and those who had been blind were gazing about them! The crowds just marveled, and praised the God of Israel" (Matthew 15:30-31, *The Living Bible*).

You and I would demand repentance before we would heal a sinner's sick body. Our God is different. He reaches out in love to those who do not deserve it: "In this is love, not that we loved

God but that he loved us and sent his Son to be the expiation for our sins" (1 John 4:10). As God's people begin to understand his method of operation, dynamic — even explosive — results follow. It is so wonderful a discovery that no one has to *deserve* God's blessings; indeed, no one ever can deserve his love.

Just as the sinful flocked to Jesus, in spite of the repeated warnings of their rabbis, so the suffering and the sinful will flock to him today. No gimmicks, no new ideas, no campaigns, no pledges, no feelings of guilt because our-church-is-not-doing-whatever-it-is-we-ought-to-be-doing — just "Jesus Christ and him crucified." When Jesus is proclaimed in the power of God's Holy Spirit, successful evangelism is the most obvious result.

What's happening at the Pittsburgh Church of the Brethren? As Philip said to Nathanel, "Come, and see." You will find here a ministry that is consciously designed after the ministry of Jesus and his apostles.

Actually, we in the Pittsburgh Church do very little, speaking in human terms. We give the hard work to the Holy Spirit. He draws the people — packing a 200-seat auditorium with up to 500. The Holy Spirit heals their bodies — how could we mere humans repair a congenital heart defect? Or remove arthritic growths from a shoulder? The Spirit of God casts out fear — he repairs broken hearts. The Holy Spirit alone convicts man of sin and his need for salvation — we humans cannot touch the heart of man.

Jesus could not possibly have attracted huge crowds of four and five thousand were it not for the power of the Holy Spirit healing the lame, blind, and deaf. Few would have come to hear him proclaim the good news otherwise. But though Jesus hid in the barren mountains of Galilee, still the throngs found their way to his hiding place. *Then* Jesus could talk of God, and *then* they listened. No advertising campaign — just a word-of-mouth message for hungry, hurting people. No promotional schemes — merely the love of God manifested in the power of the Holy Spirit.

A woman, bleeding and suffering for many years, stepped close enough to Jesus one day and his healing power surged through her body. Why can't *we* do those same things today?

Well, we can.

A Roman Catholic nun, her guitar leaning against the altar rail, announces that someone's left knee is now being healed by the Holy Spirit. Four hundred of us look at each other. No one speaks or acknowledges such a healing. Then, halfway down the center aisle, a woman slowly raises her hand. The pastor of the church carries a microphone back to ask what has happened to her.

LaVerne is obviously in some distress. With tears streaming down her cheeks, LaVerne relates a tragic story of pain and failure. "I was injured in a car accident in 1937. My left knee and ankle were badly damaged and I have had three operations in the thirty-five years since the accident. Another operation is scheduled for this summer.

"For all these years I have never been without pain, but suddenly the knee is healed! A few minutes ago it was swollen much larger than the other knee, but now it is normal for the first time! I can move it, push on it, do anything just like my right knee. It doesn't hurt anymore! Oh, praise the Lord!''

The entire congregation erupts in joyous worship of the God who loves LaVerne. Her tears flow freely as she demonstrates the use of her leg to everyone present.

I was the pastor and Sister Kristin Spell the nun. The scene occurred on a Sunday evening in our Pittsburgh Church of the Brethren. Of course, LaVerne's operation was cancelled, and to this day she bounces joyfully and gratefully on two normal legs.

LaVerne is in sales work. Her eager testimony to her customers has led others to the Sunday evening service to receive God's healing touch. But greatest of all, LaVerne through this experience came to know Jesus Christ and to find forgiveness for her sins and to receive life everlasting. LaVerne is now another ''turned-on'' Roman Catholic.

What was occurring that evening? Certainly God's power was flowing. And LaVerne surely felt loved — perhaps more loved than at any other time in her life. God's Holy Spirit, the third person of the Trinity — the *forgotten* person of the Trinity — was flowing in power across the congregation.

Yet it was not as if there were four hundred passive Christians present. Somehow, nearly everyone was actively involved. For the Holy Spirit *uses people*. And he uses people in a cooperative manner; as if to say, ''You do your part and I'll do mine." "Our part" is natural, human; but the Holy Spirit's part is *super*natural, divine. The Spirit of God mediates his supernatural life through our natural lives in what are called "gifts of the Spirit" — *charismata* in the Greek.

La Verne was freed from thirty-five years of bondage and pain through the operation of two of the Spirit's gifts — knowledge and healing.

Certainly we can do the same things Jesus did! Did he not promise? "He who believes in me will also do the works that I do, and greater works than these will he do." (John 14:12). We need only to trust the Spirit of God instead of limiting him by our fears, or unbelief, or man-developed theology.

First, our fears. We humans are afraid of the supernatural power of God. I often find so-called Christians avoiding me like the plague: they're afraid of the power of God. But why should we be frightened of our heavenly Father? He loves us and makes available the miracle-working power of his Spirit. The Holy Spirit loves us just as Jesus does.

And then there are our fears of other people — particularly those in our peer groups. We are afraid of what others will say or do. We fear losing our friends if we go "all-out" for Jesus Christ. Indeed, Jesus warned us that we would have just such problems. But he encouraged us to follow him anyway. And he is so faithful; Jesus will replace every lost friend with many new and solid friends.

Second, our unbelief. We tend to believe man rather than God. Our Father demonstrated so clearly in the gospels his will to heal everybody. To this statement unbelieving man replies, "Nonsense!" Whom will we Christians believe — God or man? Jesus could do little in his hometown because of their unbelief, and American Christians today are much like the Nazarenes of old. Worse yet, we experience such unbelief even among "fundamental" Christians.

Third, man-developed theology. So many Christians say that God doesn't work miracles today — that they ended with the apostolic age. Why do they say that? Because the Bible suggests it? Not at all. Do they not rather insist that the age of miracles is ended "because they haven't been happening in *my* life"?

Actually, "Jesus Christ is the same yesterday, today and forever." He operates today — through his Spirit — just as he did on the shores of Galilee. The evidence is overwhelming. It is so pathetic and ironic to have a man look me right in the eye and argue his doctrine of unbelief, while I am recalling having seen again and again — just the previous Sunday evening — all the miracles he insists are impossible. A man with an argument is no match for a man with an experience.

Therefore, I urge pastors and members of the Church of the Brethren not to be afraid of the power of God or "the face of man"; to believe *all* of God's promises and appropriate *all* of his powerful love; and to ignore the unbiblical teachings that are abroad in the church. Let's get on with our Father's business!

Now, evangelism is not merely building membership rolls, Sunday school attendance or stewardship results. Evangelism is speaking effectively to men about Jesus Christ and him crucified.

Every pastor should first ask himself, "Am *I* really saved from my sins? Do *I* know Jesus Christ personally?" It is useless for pastors to speak of evangelism unless they first commit themselves to Jesus Christ. Not to the church, but a commitment to *Jesus* as "Boss" — our own personal Lord of life.

"Collectivizing" the gospel is a cruel unbiblical joke. Every man must make a personal decision for Jesus. And when the man in the pulpit accepts Jesus as his own "Boss," others will inevitably follow from the pews. The church will start "being the church."

Every man must hear, in terms that speak to him personally, that Jesus Christ died, taking the punishment for *our* sins on himself. Then he should be faced with a call to repent of sin and accept Jesus Christ. This is evangelism.

But how do we get a man's attention in this helter-skelter age? Man is busy running to and fro — going nowhere but downhill to destruction. And he is so busy doing it that he won't stop to hear the message of salvation in Jesus Christ.

Here is where the Holy Spirit comes in. A large segment of this hectic humanity hurts — hurts badly. Their bodies are racked with pain; emotionally they are coming apart at the seams; and spiritually they feel a great, big, empty hole somewhere deep within them.

We *can* reach sinful man — at the point where he hurts, at the level where his foundations are crumbling, and at the heart of that yawning void within him. But we have got to use the mighty power of God's Holy Spirit to accomplish this task. Just as Jesus got the attention of a whole nation with his miracles so we can do it. He promised.

Brethren, let's be done with theological quibbling based on human logic and face God's word honestly and without embarrassment. Let's end the perpetual search for new methods and concentrate on the reliable methods the New Testament so graphically portrays.

"And he called to him his twelve disciples and gave them authority over unclean spirits, to cast them out, and to heal every disease and every infirmity. . . . These twelve Jesus sent out, charging them, . . . 'Preach as you go, saying, "The kingdom of heaven is at hand." Heal the sick, raise the dead, cleanse lepers, cast out demons'" (Matthew 10:1, 5a, 7-8a).

We *can* do it!

The best news comes to us in Jesus Christ and makes things happen! . . . Things happen because the Holy Spirit provides the impetus for power and action. As a person is filled continually with God's Spirit, he is motivated to use all his gifts to channel the best news.

From: *A Statement on Evangelism,* Annual Conference, 1972

C. Wayne Zunkel *has been pastor of the Elizabethtown Church of the Brethren in Pennsylvania since 1969. Prior to that he served for thirteen years as pastor of the First Church in Harrisburg, Pennsylvania. During his ministry there, the church developed a seven-day-a-week program to relate to its community, including an after-school club program, day care center, and a fellowship house. He is a member of the General Board of his denomination, having served as chairman of the Parish Ministries Commission, and a member of the Executive Committee. An active participant in the ecumenical movement, Wayne Zunkel has been a member of the General Board of the National Council of Churches and chairman of the Brethren delegation. He also served as president of the Council of Churches of Greater Harrisburg and of the United Churches of Elizabethtown. He was for six years chairman of the Legislative Committee of the Pennsylvania Council of Churches. He is moderator of the "Face the Issue" radio program currently broadcast on five area stations.*

The High Cost of a Cheap Faith

C. Wayne Zunkel

During three of my four years in college I sang in the college choir. In those days we traveled to concerts in cars. The driver for the group with which I was assigned was a black student from Chicago, a Roman Catholic, a good student, cultured, handsome, interesting to be with.

As we traveled with him we heard many of the comments he faced from members of some of the white churches in which we sang. Not mean comments, just curious comments, as if because of the pigmentation of his skin he was somehow different. Their naive curiosity was rude and cutting.

One Sunday night as we were returning to the college after singing in a church, a well-known evangelist was on the radio. My friend, Wes, left the program on. It was raining. The roads were slippery, the visibility was poor. We came to a traffic light. The car ahead stopped suddenly. Wes saw what was happening but was not able to come to a complete stop in time and rather unceremoniously bumped the car ahead. It seemed rather obvious that no damage was done, but he got out in the driving rain to talk to the driver who happened to be white. We heard the other driver tear into Wes seemingly not so much because he could not stop in time, but basically because he was black. Wes said little. He stood there and took it.

When he got back into the car, the evangelist on the radio was still preaching away. Wes heard him out. Then he turned off the radio and said quietly, "The trouble with people like that is, all that matters is that you 'Come to Jesus.' It doesn't matter how you treat a person like me."

More than simply being irrelevent, for many people "evangelism" has actually been bad news. The word "evangel" in the New Testament means "the good news." But for some, when they are finished with it, it comes out quite another way.

A Mennonite tract entitled *Evangelism: Good News or Bad News,* notes, "It's not easy to make bad news out of news as good as God's love in Christ. But there have always been Christians equal to the task."

An "infidel Turk" in 1095 discovered that "the peace of God" which the Crusades delivered to Jerusalem was brought on the edge of a sword, and it hardly seemed good news.

In the thirteenth-century Inquisition, the gospel spelled bad news if you were adjudged guilty of deviation because your understanding of God's word was different from those in authority.

For the Mindanao tribesmen of the Philippines, the Christian settler's submachine guns speak instant news — "No room for primitives!" For the Black Zulu, white Christian *apartheid* is neither good nor news.

Many people say accepting Christ is a kind of two-step process. First, you give your life to God. Then, if you have given your life to God, good works, a clean life, ethical concern and morality will follow. But even to say that, is to suggest that there can be a step one without a step two.

The little band of "confessing Christians" in Germany who opposed Hitler faced this kind of logic and knew its tragic results. So many Christians in Germany, like so many Christians in our day and in our land, believed that having their hearts right with God was a separate issue from the ethics or morality of their lives. As a result many Catholics, Lutherans, and Mennonites in Germany supported Hitler overwhelmingly. They saw no relationship between their personal affairs and the affairs of the state.

One who was outspoken in his opposition to the acquiescence of German churchmen to obvious evil was Dietrich Bonhoeffer. His book, *The Cost of Discipleship,* spells out the reasons for his opposition. He begins by talking about "cheap grace," the concept that God's love for us, once we accept him, overlooks what we are and do. Bonhoeffer says what is needed is "costly grace." He says,

"The only one who has a right to say that he is justified by grace alone is the person who has left all to follow Christ."

He says the call goes out today, just as it went to the disciples long ago. Jesus says, now as then, "Come follow" and the response of disciples is a single act of obedience, a willingness to turn around and go with him. It is not a matter of two steps but of one.

The New Testament does not separate what we do from what we believe or what we are. They are bound together in one package. Indeed, the New Testament acknowledges that what we do is rooted firmly in what we are. Jesus says it bluntly, "A bad tree cannot produce good fruit. Nor does a sound tree produce bad fruit. By their fruits you shall know them." "You don't gather grapes from thorns nor figs from thistles" (Matthew 7:16-20). "If you love me, you will keep my commandments." "If anyone says, 'I love God,' and hates his brother, he is a liar; for he who does not love his brother whom he has seen, cannot love God whom he has not seen" (1 John 4:20).

This is not a response of first the mind, then the mouth, and finally a response of heart and hands, but one response of a total life, for Christ or against him. Jesus says, "Come, live with me, learn of me, walk with me, live in my way." And either we go or we refuse to go. It is that simple.

The story I like best to describe it is the story of the tightrope walker who had a cable stretched across Niagara Falls and was scheduled to push a man in a wheelbarrow across it. Early that morning, a crowd had gathered. He walked up to one of the people in the crowd, and he said, "Do you believe I can do this?" The person said, "Yes, I believe you can do it." "Good," said the tightrope artist, "the person who was to ride in the wheelbarrow didn't show up. You'll be the one." And the mist of the spray of the water was on his face and the roar of the river pounding on the rocks far below filled the air.

To believe is more than a matter of the mind. If we believe, we will go with Jesus in a single act of the mind and of the will.

A CHEAP faith is terribly expensive. We've seen its high, high cost across the years. We saw it in the early history of our own country when Christians dealt in the slave trade. Slave ships had human beings chained together row after row with only a few feet separating one row from the row above it. There in the human excreta and heat many died. And the dead were left chained to the living. Cattle would not be shipped that way. Cattle at least have room to stand. Families were deliberately separated. It was a cruel, heartless business to be in.

One of the leaders in that cruel business was John Newton, captain of one of those slave ships, who wrote five of the hymns in our hymnal, including, "How Sweet the Name of Jesus Sounds," "Amazing Grace," and "Glorious Things of Thee Are Spoken." He held public worship for his crew of thirty twice every Sunday. The first slave ship to land in Jamestown in 1619 was named "Jesus." Because of countless examples like that Christianity has been discredited in the eyes of many people around the world. Christians have often twisted the Bible and blasphemed their Lord in an attempt to separate doing from believing.

There is a single line from the English poet Swinburne which says it best for me: "For tender minds they served up half a Christ." Since the first century, there are Christians who have been at work trying to do that.

There are Christians who have had the notion that they can love God and have his favor while they have contempt for those who are his children. It just cannot be that way.

The other extreme is just as inadequate and just as dangerous. Some think they can buy into the action side of the gospel, the social concern, the humanitarian emphasis, without relating to the God who ties it all together. They want social action without personal commitment.

A Brethren leader who used to teach sociology at a Brethren college commented recently on second thoughts he has about his approach in the classroom. He talked about some of his students of just a few years back who went out of his classroom into the world fired up to work at social change but who today are burned out, cynical, withdrawn. He said he shared his social concerns with them but failed in the classroom to adequately share the basic Christian motivation and source of power which led him to those concerns and sustained him in them. Because of the pressures of secularism upon our educational systems, even in a church-related college, he had succumbed at times to serving up "half a Christ" — the social concern for people apart from the context of the

God in whom it all takes on meaning and in whom there is hope.

In a booklet I did some years ago, *Why Brethren,* writing in a chapter, "Is Christianity Personal or Social?" I talked of flying to Portland, Oregon, for a meeting of the General Board of the National Council of Churches with a minister whom Special Assistant to President Johnson, Bill Moyers, one time had said was more responsible than any other person in America for the passage of significant civil rights legislation in that period. He was an articulate churchman, a brilliant man. I wrote that this minister sipped his Bloody Mary and I my tomato juice as we talked about the church's necessary involvement in society's big problems.

But this eloquent, fearless, perceptive spokesman on the question of civil rights, a giant of a man with a great social consciousness, had bought half a faith. Like so many Christians in our day, he believed Christianity was either personal or social, and for him it was clearly, dynamically social. But in his personal life, where faith did not have the same kind of clear, definitive claim, he was a troubled, guilt-ridden, tormented, driven man. Behind the scenes, there was a pattern of sordid confusion, guilt, and fear. In the end, people close to him said, he was murdered in a lonely hotel room, probably by a man with a driving hunger for sex. A great man at one level, twisted and troubled at another level.

Or I think of some of the social giants in the peace movement. A well-known churchman was a saint in many people's eyes. But his self-indulgence and failure in terms of high personal standards made his ringing words suddenly seem hollow and empty. His once avid followers became disillusioned and bitter. Then came the news that his wife, also a leader in the peace movement, was arrested and was convicted on shoplifting charges in a suburban department store.

In an Old Testament phrase is the discovery that "Our gods have clay feet" (Daniel 2:33). Those mortals we worship who seem gods of silver or gold with bodies of iron do have weaknesses which can bring them tumbling down.

We all sin. And it is unfair to discredit anyone because of areas of failure. We all fail.

The tragedy is when we have a theology, an inderstanding of faith which *invites* failure. When, because of blindness, we say, "Half the gospel matters but the other half is unimportant." When we advocate, when we teach, expect, seek failure in one area — without knowing that such shortsightedness on our part will cancel out our most noble dreams.

Too long the world has suffered from people who consider themselves Christian but who go into the world with half a faith — half a Christ. For too long Christians have been divided into two camps. Those who believe in *personal salvation* on one side and, on the other, those who believe in the *social gospel.* But the Bible does not know the terms "personal salvation" or "social gospel." Salvation means wholeness. The gospel means good news. And that wholeness and that good news is at the same time both social and personal. It touches every area of life.

Christ calls us to nothing less than the *full gospel* — the whole gospel for the whole person in the whole world.

Why is it that those with a half gospel are often so much more enthusiastic than those who have a vision of the full range of Christ's teaching? Civil rights leaders will gladly lay down their lives for their cause. Anti-war activists will gladly forsake all, go to prison, face untold hardships, give up their most valued earthly possession, their U. S. citizenship and flee to Canada. On the other side, we see so-called "fundamentalists" risking personal abuse, ridicule, or shame as they witness for their purely personal Christ. Fundamentalist students on a college campus will invite harsh attacks for their faith.

Both those for whom the gospel is only social action and those for whom it is only personal salvation give to their faith with devotion and creativity. Why is it that so often those with their hands on both reins of the gospel, who have it in perspective and balance, don't seem to care as much?

Jesus said the sons of this world are so much wiser in their own generation than the sons of light (Luke 16:8). Why is it that those with half a Christ sometimes seem to care more, share more, invest more of themselves than those with a vision of the full Christ and the totality of his demands?

Roy Forney, the former minister of visitation at our church, asked me what I thought of Billy Graham's film, *Time to Run*. I enjoyed it. It was the moving story of a young man and his family who were running away from themselves and from

God. In the end, they "come to themselves."

After I had babbled on about it for awhile, I asked Roy what he thought. His comment was a single sentence: "It stopped where it should have started."

And that's true! It stopped with some people making a change in their lives. It portrayed the impact of that change but relayed none of the content, none of the implications of what it means to turn life over to God. It stopped where it should have started.

It occurs to me that so many efforts which label themselves as "evangelism" are that way.

Roy went on to share a story about Ralph Schlosser, a former professor and a former president of Elizabethtown College, also a beloved preacher in our parts. Dr. Schlosser was baptizing a 60-year-old man. When he had finished, the man looked up at Brother Schlosser and said in German, "Thank God, it's over now." But Ralph Schlosser replied in German, "No, my friend, it's just beginning." Many Christians are so concerned about the *new birth* that they spend little energy or attention on *growing up*.

On one side are actionists who are content that another person catches a glimpse of opposition to war or involvement in civil rights or equal justice. They don't want to risk losing that newfound social concern in another person by muddying the water trying to give some theological or Biblical undergirding to what has happened.

At the other extreme are those who focus on a warm, personal experience of God, yet are fearful that any rounding out of the faith might frighten people off, turn them away from a personal acceptance of Jesus and a personal knowledge of God. So they avoid talking about the gospel's social implications.

The Apostle Paul had words for those who wanted to keep newborn Christians forever on milk, never letting them sink their teeth into the meat and potatoes of the gospel (1 Cor. 3:1-2).

My own conviction is that not until we cut loose the ties to mundane things and become participants in full discipleship, not until then will we know the fire in our lives which no one can contain (Luke 12:49). For when that fire comes, it will be shared! None can hold it within. When it comes, it consumes the one who carries it in his heart and it leaps the boundaries of personality. It spreads like a late summer forest fire in a dry and thirsty land.

Then we become as wise as serpents and as innocent as doves (Matthew 10:16). Then we rack our imaginations to find new and more powerful ways to share the faith which has possessed us. Then evangelism becomes not a duty, not an un-unwanted task, not a source of guilt and concern or of special conferences on evangelism, but a way of life which we spread as surely as we pass on the measles if we have caught them.

True evangelism is as natural as shouting to the world that *we are in love*. For that is what we are: in love with God, in love with our friend Jesus who has introduced us to the Father, in love with our brothers and our sisters, in love with life itself. And in that condition we can do no other than to witness to what we have seen and heard.

David S. Young *is in his fourth year as pastor of the Bush Creek Church of the Brethren in Maryland, a ministry he undertook soon after his graduation from Bethany Theological Seminary. A native of Hanover, Pennsylvania, and a graduate of Elizabethtown College, he recently enrolled in the beginning year of the Doctor of Ministry program at Bethany. He has already given leadership in interchurch activities, having served as the coordinator for Key '73 in Frederick County, Maryland, and as a past president of Frederick Churches United. Youngest of the contributors to this volume, he lists his current enthusiasms as biblical studies, adult education, and the renewal of faith in persons and churches. David and Joan Young are the parents of a son, Jonathan Matthew, born in January 1972.*

Lay Witness-- Road to Renewal

10

David Young

The Bush Creek congregation in Maryland will never be the same. The Lay Witness Mission in which our local church participated recently has brought about profound changes in the life of our congregation. This was my initial feeling when, as pastor, I observed the Witness at first-hand. It is still my feeling months after it happened.

My wife, Joan, puts it this way. She recalled that when we remodeled our church a couple of years ago, the pews were turned around. But as a result of the Lay Witness weekend, she says, "The church was turned around."

And so it was, because persons began to experience what real Christian community can be. Lives were fundamentally changed as people met Christ through the love and sharing of a group of alive Christians. It was like experiencing a resurrection in our own midst. There was an awesome wonder that it was all really happening, like the feeling of the disciples who saw the empty tomb — almost too good to be true. The weekend left me with the feeling that within our congregation there would be a lot more praying and a deeper fellowship, affirming the love of God and love for one another.

What is a Lay Witness mission? It centers in a weekend experience in a local church in which members of other congregations come and share their faith. These witnesses come at their own expense, often over great distances. They share in the simplest possible way. They are not specially trained nor do they try to be professional. All of them have experienced similar missions in their own churches. Coming from every walk of life, these representatives are lay persons who are seeking ever more fully to understand the Christian way.

Our church was cautious in considering having a Lay Witness Mission. At first it was hard for us to see just how the events of such a weekend would fit together. And that word *witness* — what would these people say? Would they give us pat answers? Would they deal with realistic questions? And would we be able to find enough volunteers to serve on the some fourteen committees as suggested in the preparation manual, *A Road to Renewal?*

With great faith our church board voted to have the Lay Witness Mission. The chairman of the deacons sent the application form in, and the Lay Renewal Institute assigned a coordinator. Representatives from our church met with him to discuss the responsibilities of each committee. At that time we decided also to have the youth and the children's witness. Slowly committees began to form and to set timetables for the work involved.

The amount of effort was tremendous: sending out invitations, finding housing for thirty-eight guests, planning meals, setting up neighborhood coffee groups, and informing everyone of the weekend — to name the most urgent jobs. Enthusiasm was generated, but there were several low points. We wanted to have a twenty-four-hour prayer vigil just prior to the weekend. The prayer committee struggled to get the prayer chart filled with volunteers until the very day before the vigil. Altogether, some ninety people pulled together to make this weekend possible.

And then it happened. Witnesses began arriving Friday afternoon. There were the initial greetings and an abundance of laughter. The coordinator invited all team members to a meeting and, doing what seemed impossible, pulled that group of almost total strangers together, explaining the purposes of the weekend, offering guidelines, and assigning responsibilities. The session ended with a prayer, and the team went downstairs for the fellowship meal.

As pastor I was aware that our people were still

a bit anxious over whether many persons from our congregation would be present. But all of the 175 chairs which we had set up in faith were full. The meal was tasty and the food was abundant. Then the coordinator called on the first witness to share. A big strong man weighing at least 215 pounds went to the front. He asked someone to pray for him as he began to speak. He said, "I am Bill Drumheller. I am an alcoholic."

Bill went on to tell how faith in Christ changed his life. He made it quite clear that he is an alcoholic, not that he was one. The desire is still there even after many years of being dry, but Bill told us how Christ continually helps him cope with this desire.

After other witnesses were called on to share, the congregation broke up into small groups with two witnesses assigned to each of them. We expressed our hopes about what would happen in our lives and in the life of the church over that weekend. Barriers began to come down; people shared honestly as to where they were in their lives. Some groups stopped on time; others stayed together long after they were dismissed. We all went home tired, but with a sense that something important was happening.

The Saturday program began with a team meeting at the church. Witnesses then dispersed to homes in the congregation where coffee groups were held. The total church was drawn back together for lunch, after which there were men's and women's groups. Again in the evening there was a congregational meal. A genuine spirit of oneness was developing. The youth too shared their talents and witnessed to their faith. The personal sharing continued in small groups throughout the evening. Late Saturday night the sanctuary was open for prayer. Witnesses prayed with people about situations they were facing in their own lives.

On Sunday morning the church was filled with people. Witnesses again shared their faith. The coordinator offered a very low-key invitation for a rededication of life to Christ. Those who responded filled the front of the church, then the center aisle and side aisles. New commitments were made, tears flowed, people embraced. Many went downstairs for the farewell dinner. We ended by joining in a large circle to sing the song, "Pass It On." Goodbyes were not easy. Persons from the congregation who could stay for the evaluation were overwhelmed and grateful for what had happened. Each one had his own unique experience, a different encounter. All had found new friends.

THE AFTERMATH of the Lay Witness weekend is also part of the story. Many persons had gained new understanding of their faith and wanted to pursue the search for its meaning. People began to feel that their lives were important to Christ and to others. One witness with whom many could identify said she had read a story about cactus plants. Some varieties of cactus bloom once a year and one might miss it if it isn't observed at the right time. "That's the way my life is," she said. "I bloom once in a great while and the blossom might be missed." This simple kind of sharing of the faith in unadorned fashion encouraged life-changing for many people. It affirmed for many that God uses the gifts of even very ordinary persons.

Another aftermath is evident in the significance of small groups. Our church had prevously developed several small groups, but after the lay witness experience they took on a new character and depth. Groups now have the motivation to work at new relationships and to grow in faith.

Soon after this some of our people received invitations to go from our congregation as witnesses to other churches. For this purpose a training program is provided by the Lay Renewal Institute. An innovation on our part has been a reentry session for witnesses. Through the process of helping another church in renewal, witnesses come back renewed themselves.

Since our lay witness experience, prayer has become much more real in the congregation. An individual member does not hesitate to call someone and say, "Pray for me." Frequently in a conversation you will hear someone say, "I will pray for you." People have commented freely about the results of prayer. There is a renewed sense of God's working among his people.

Finally, there is a new level of caring for people inside and outside our congregation. People are trying to relate to others. There are new efforts to understand each person and to help each other. A natural follow-up of the lay witness emphasis has been the strengthening of the social ministries of the church, caring for the physical needs of those outside our own fellowship.

For MANY congregations the lay witness movement will strike a new note in evangelism. It is based on persons simply and directly sharing their faith and love. The word *witness* itself implies relating a firsthand experience. Too often we have thought of a witness as a person who gives a five-minute testimonial that has already been shared many times. The emphasis in the lay witness movement is on relating our faith in Christ with our daily struggles. It is similar to the picture of early Christians who experienced a meaningful faith and then shared it. Faith becomes a first person reality so needed in this day when we struggle with the practices that too often have become empty forms. Evangelism is natural to the lay witness style of life. It is intentional, yet not superficial or pushy or seasonal.

Perhaps the greatest discovery of the Lay Witness Mission for evangelism and the church is the recognition that people everywhere are hungering for faith by which to live. We all need nourishment for our faith daily. The servant posture of the church, which has been emphasized in recent years, is but one of the needs. All of us need the living bread. The church must help persons who are hungering for the vital faith that will give an answer the meaning to life; the faith that will provide a feeling of security so that there will be energy to risk; the faith that will deal with authority so that we know where we belong and where we are going. Evangelism points to the central convictions that nourish us as Christians and keep us moving.

Art Gish *is an itinerant preacher who spends much* of his time traveling *with his family across the* country speaking *to churches and schools and* sometimes in the streets. *He is the author of* The New Left and Christian Radicalism *and* Beyond the Rat Race *and is currently writing a book* on Christian community. *He is a contributing editor to* The Other Side *and* The Post American. *A graduate of Manchester College and Bethany Theological Seminary, Art Gish was in Brethren Volunteer Service in Europe and has worked extensively in the civil rights and peace movements in this country. He is especially interested in the Brethren heritage and the recovery of the Anabaptist vision. With his wife and three children, he lives in Philadelphia where his family are members of an intentional Christian community.*

Called to a Covenant Community

Art Gish

If we had a New Testament-based evangelism, what shape would it take? What would evangelism look like, Anabaptist style? The questions are important not only for the identity of Brethren, but the answers could well determine whether or not our witness will be faithful to our Lord, his gospel and his kingdom. It is important that our evangelism be an authentic expression of our faith and not a borrowed method expressing a theology foreign to our own.

One of the marks of the believers' church tradition is not only a deep concern for witness, but also the understanding that the Great Commission is binding on all believers in every age. The missionary mandate applies to all Christians, not only to certain trained specialists. It is an active program of evangelism that makes a voluntary church possible. Without it, we soon settle back into an establishment church which relies primarily on baptizing its children and devising political strategies to sustain itself.

Not only do Christians have a mandate for evangelism, but the condition of the world demands it. Even creation is groaning for its redemption. With the world going to hell and our knowing the way to salvation, it is unthinkable that we would not be sharing and proclaiming that good news to the whole world. There is a real urgency about spreading the Word. It is essential that people come into right relation with God. Without God we are lost.

But what is this gospel, this good news? Obviously it is not inviting people to join our nice church, projecting a good image or blessing society's values. Neither is it offering free tickets to heaven with a full fire insurance policy included. It is not pacifism or even primarily calling people to accept forgiveness for their sins.

The good news is that God loves us and seeks to save us, that in Jesus Christ the powers of sin and death have been defeated, that a new kingdom has come and is coming in which we can already participate.

Evangelism then is more than getting someone to accept some new ideas or even to believe in Jesus. Evangelism is the call to reorient one's whole life because of what God has done in Jesus Christ and is doing now in our midst, a call to

reorient one's whole life to the coming of the kingdom. This includes the reminder that the only
way to enter the kingdom is to renounce all that
one has, a complete commitment and surrender
of all to Jesus Christ.

Evangelism is confronting people with the gospel
of Jesus Christ and challenging them to accept it.
It is calling people to repent, to turn from their
old life of slavery in sin to a new life of liberation
in Christ, calling alienated and lost people into the
fellowship of the new creation. Nothing less will
do.

Evangelism is witnessing to Jesus Christ, but
this does not mean any christ. Not the christ who
blesses wars, supports racism and condones greed
for money and power. Not just an inner christ,
not an Americanized, protestantized christ. No,
it is the living Christ of the New Testament who
both calls us to a totally new life and gives us the
power to live it.

Hopefully our concern for evangelism grows
out of the reality of the gospel in our lives rather
than the fact that so many people are talking about
it or that we desire to increase our membership.
The first question is not action or program, but
being, Spirit and commitment. The need is not
to come up with a better program of evangelism,
but to get ourselves together, to be faithful and in
tune with the Spirit, and then correct action can
follow.

Unless we are living it, there will be little
power in our message. The gospel is believable
only as it is expressed by a community which is

demonstrating it. Our most important witness is in our being, in the life-style of the Christian community. Do we love each other and our enemies? Do we demonstrate a visible, alternative way of life? Can the kingdom be seen breaking into our midst? A visible church is required for a visible witness to the world. The church must have integrity and discipline before it can witness with any authority.

We do not need a new program of evangelism. *We need a revival!* Until our congregations become communities of love, until we begin again to practice Matthew 18:15-20, until our lives together are centered on Christ's kingdom, there will be no evangelism worth discussing. The first need is a rebirth of our congregations. When the book of Acts records great works in the early church it reminds us that they were "of one mind and one accord." They were living it.

Jesus said we *are,* not should be, the salt of the earth, the light of the world. By our very nature we *are*. What can light do other than shine? Being light is its own witness to darkness. A healthy tree *will,* not should, produce fruit. If love exists in the community it cannot help but shine on those outside the community.

The more deeply we experience community and Christ's kingdom the more we long for its fulfilment in the world. The more we experience liberation and victory over sin the more we see the need to struggle against the forces of death and evil everywhere. The more we experience God's love the more eager and willing we will be to reach out and care for others. Our witness comes out of our existence, a natural expression of our new life in Christ. The point is not that we believe Christian teachings are the best, but that we have come to know the power of Jesus Christ in our congregations.

Our best witness is not our words, but our changed lives, the new creation in our midst, a community that people can taste and see. Our witness is being a new humanity in which all our social relationships demonstrate to the world how life is to be lived. The community embodies in its life the solution to war, hunger, alienation, strife, oppression — and whatever other problems haunt our world.

Not only is it important that we live and be what we preach, but also that we be sent into mission by the Holy Spirit. The Spirit who gathers us together is the same Spirit who sends us out. We cannot go, however, before we are sent. There are times a community needs to stop its activity and wait to receive power and be sent.

A desire to serve or a concern for the lost is not enough qualification to do God's work. One must be called and sent. The Holy Spirit did not allow Paul and Silas to go to Bithynia (Acts 16:6-7), but sent them instead to Troas. We should not plan our mission and then pray for God's help to complete it. We do not decide what our mission should be or choose a mission, but we need to be open for the Spirit to give us a mission. Mission is a gift of God.

Evangelism includes a call to discipleship, to live in Christ's kingdom rather than the kingdoms of this world. Discipleship is more than the result of the gospel; it is an essential aspect of the gospel. Christ is not only a way *to* life, but also a way *of* life. When we call people to commit their lives to Jesus Christ, we must remind them that their whole lives need to come under his Lordship.

In the New Testament there is no offer of cheap grace. Justification is for the sinner, not for sin. Salvation is not free; it costs us our lives. The gospel is not only relational; it includes norms, values and expectations. Evangelism is a call to discipleship, not an easy appeasing of people's consciences. More is expected than "only believe." The gospel relates to people's lives, and to such matters as sex, economics, education, or politics. In every activity of life Christ stands as Lord and Judge.

Evangelism includes a call to repentance, without which there can be no salvation. And those calls to repentance need to be specific and concrete. Conversion means more than "peace in my heart." It includes also a demand that my life be changed. We cannot ask if it is more important to be forgiven for stealing or to stop stealing. The two cannot be separated.

The old Brethren were very wise in their rejection of shallow evangelistic programs. So often mass evangelism is an accommodation to the spirit and values of the present age, bringing more unregenerate people into the church, making the church even more apostate than before.

Rather than watering down the demands of the gospel to the point where the largest number can be included, we must make clear the demands of the cross, even if this means that no one will accept the call. Brothers and sisters, may we never ask persons to commit their lives to Christ without informing them of what that involves. Ask them first to count the cost.

If our emphasis is on discipleship, we will not call people to be saved, but rather preach that salvation is a gift of God which comes to us as we renounce sin and our loyalties to the old order and false gods. As we make that break and commit ourselves to Christ we experience the new birth and salvation. Many who preach "get saved," insist on a personal commitment before they talk about discipleship assuming that such questions as participation in war or racism will take care of themselves. Yet seldom do these people ever get to the concerns of discipleship. But calling people to Christ means calling them to discipleship.

T HE ISSUE in evangelism is whether our witness is faithfully made without compromise in the face of either apathy, opposition or eager acceptance. Our witness is judged not by the subjective response of individuals, but by whether it is faithful to the character and message of Jesus Christ, to whom our witness should always point.

We dare not tone down the revolutionary aspects of the gospel, nor may we avoid everything controversial. If the church truly preached the gospel, this whole country would shake and tremble. But that gospel is not being preached. Personal salvation is being preached, the social gospel is talked about, there is talk of going back to the Bible and an outpouring of the Spirit, but the gospel is not being preached with power.

Evangelism relates to the reality of sin. The early Christians saw themselves engaged in a cosmic, mortal struggle with the forces of evil. They knew they were wrestling "not against flesh and blood, but against principalities, against powers, against the rulers of the darkness of this world, against spiritual wickedness in high places" Galations 6:12). Our evangelism must come to grips with the power of sin in the world and confront those powers with the atoning work of Jesus Christ.

The preaching of the gospel will include condemnation of sin. Every evangelist has a list of sins. Evangelists are well known for their preaching against the sins of adultery, drinking, and stealing. Developing conviction regarding sin is considered one important aspect of evangelism. Is it not strange that in a century of world wars and the threat of nuclear holocaust so few preachers have been willing to include war in their list of sins, to say nothing of racism, exploitation, and greed? Why does their list not also include militarism, imperialism, and nationalism?

While the early revivalism in the nineteenth century proclaimed the Lordship of Christ over all of life and was not afraid to deal with social issues, later revivalism, directed by its smooth evangelists, was careful not to offend the rich and powerful from whom they received their money and instead concentrated on the sins of the working class.

The New Testament says that when the gospel was preached the poor heard it gladly. Today we

seem to have a message that the rich hear more
gladly than the poor. Maybe we need to take another look at our message. How does it come
across to the poor, the downtrodden, the despised?
All too often it comes across as oppression, ratio-
nalization for exploitation, justification of the
status quo, as bad news rather than good news, as
slavery rather than liberation.

T HE CHURCH is called to be a reconciler, but that
does not mean that the role of the church is primarily to be a mediator. We must speak the truth,
and often that will bring to the surface great
amounts of hostility, hatred and sometimes even
violence. Attacking the demons is a serious matter.
The gospel does cause offense. A sinful world does
not want to hear about a righteous God. Sometimes the church will be a polarizing force in the
world. Jesus came not to bring peace, but a sword.
Without repentance and the cross there can be no
reconciliation. Reconciliation is not cheap.

At times our witness may need to be in areas
where we are unwanted. Because we are rejected is
no sufficient reason to quit, although we need to
discern when to shake the dust off our shoes and
not throw pearls to swine.

In the book of Acts people heard a message that
convicted them and called them to a new life.
There was transforming power in that message.
Do we have a message that can speak to people's
condition? Do we have a message that can cut to
the heart of America's sin? Do we have any sure
word from the Lord? The work of evangelism cannot be left to those who reduce the gospel to cheap

grace and the baptizing of American culture. We are called to preach the uncompromising gospel.

We are not called to save souls. That is the work of the Holy Spirit. Our only task is to witness. Evangelism is sowing seed. After the seed is planted, we can only humbly and hopefully wait for God to quicken the seed. We know that we cannot convict and convert, but that the Spirit through the Word can. So often our evangelism reveals a lack of faith in God. Since we are not sure God can do his work, we try to do his work for him.

There are no shortcuts to the conversion of the whole world, not by coercion, not by psychological manipulation, not by resorting to Madison Avenue organizational and technological expertise to blitz the nation for God. To the extent we believe in God we will reject gimmicks and not bait people with either guilt or the promise of extraordinary rewards.

Evangelism need not be a violation of others' dignity and freedom. Rather than being coercive or manipulative, Christian evangelism gives others the opportunity and freedom to decide for or against Christ. Evangelism means making Christian commitment a genuine option for others. Not to give them this choice is to limit their freedom.

Neither evangelicals with their preoccupation with the individual nor liberals with their preoccupation with changing structures have given much serious thought to the importance of the covenant community (the church) in the task of evangelism. Evangelism includes calling people to be a part of a new community drawn together and redeemed by Jesus Christ. God's primary work in the world is not in changing individuals or power structures, but in creating such a covenant community, the church, through which both are transformed. Evangelism then is not saving individual souls or changing the structures of society, or even some combination of the two, but calling people into a new community with all its implications for transformed persons and liberated social relationships.

Without community, evangelism makes little sense. How can we reach out to the lost if there is no faithful community to call them into and no example shown of what the new life in Christ might look like. Unless we have congregations which will be able to nurture new Christians we will bring into the church a group of spiritual children who will remain children the rest of their lives. People need a lot of help in growing into mature faith and discipleship.

The church everywhere is in a missionary situation. No longer can we presuppose the existence of a Christian society. That means evangelism and witness is involved in all of our relationships with the world.

What should you do? Go tell the world that God is and that he loves and cares, that he knows our sin and the guilt we feel, that he knows our despair, oppression and lostness. Tell people that their debt is already paid, the bondage of sin has been broken and that there is hope. Tell them that God is waiting to include them in his new community.

 **Matthew M. Meyer,** *after a thirteen-year pastorate at the Glendale Church of the Brethren in California, in 1969 became a member of the Parish Ministries Commission staff of the Church of the Brethren General Board, serving as consultant for evangelism. His parish experiences, which included a remarkable program of community services, have become an excellent resource for his significant leadership in the development of evangelistic emphases in districts as well as local congregations across the nation. He has also been his denomination's representative to the National Committee for Key '73. An accomplished singer and guitar player, he has made a unique contribution to many new expressions of contemporary worship.*

Reach Out to Share God's Love

12

Matthew M. Meyer

Out of my memory of recent years several pictures appear:

● It is a Wednesday evening prayer meeting to which a thousand chanting, clapping, young people have come to sing and rejoice, to hear simple and clear Bible teachings, to witness and to be witnessed unto, to pray, to be healed, and to make life commitments to Jesus. The atmosphere is alive and expressive and expectant.

● A twenty-two year-old gang leader stands before a Brethren congregation. He tries to speak but finds that he cannot. Later he described his experience by saying, "I got up there and saw all those good Christian people, and God hit me in the face with no words." With the aid of the pastor his words did finally flow and he spoke of his homeless and explosive experiences. "If it hadn't been for the Brethren Youth Center I'd be in jail right now. We came to tear the place apart, and we were doing just that, until we started talking to the minister here. Soon we became a part of the Brethren Youth Center." The church had taken the hands of youth to steady them through a few difficult and troublesome years. It was saving them from considerable hell.

● Ten people are meeting in a circle on a Tuesday evening as they have done for ten weeks. There is a close, warm, caring atmosphere. A kleenex box is on the table in the middle of the group. One person speaks, "I've never experienced anything like this before. I've never before felt so close to people and so accepted and affirmed. Because of this group, I'm no longer ashamed of my feelings or afraid to deal with them. Because of you, God is real to me and life has taken on new meaning."

● It is Sunday evening and 400 youth have gathered in the barn on an Eastern Pennsylvania farm. The bales of hay provide tiered seating in a small arena. The spirited singing, the freely expressed praises to God, the earnest prayers, and the personal accounts of what God is doing in individual lives, all provide a rich spiritual experience for the participants.

● It is a weekday evening. The Brethren sanctuary is packed with a strange mixture of people. Some are Christian from a variety of Protestant churches. Some are Roman Catholics, and some are Jews. Some are officers of the American Nazi Party, and some are vocal members of the John Birch Society. They have come to hear two black speakers talk about racial discrimination in the local community. The situation is volatile. The air is filled with anger and fear with occasionally a trace of hope that some communication can build a bridge across the chasm that separates the various groups of people. Tomorrow's newspaper headline will declare the success of the meeting: "Demonstration Unneeded."

● A man and his wife are visiting an elderly man in his home. They have come representing the local Church of the Brethren. In the course of the conversation they share reasons why they find regular, corporate worship an indispensable part of their week's schedule. Also they speak of what difference their faith in Christ makes in their daily lives. An invitation is extended through the question, "Mr. Larsen, have you ever considered giving your life to Christ and becoming a Christian?" Through moist eyes the old man slowly responds, "You know, I've been around a long time. I've done a lot of living, and no one has ever asked me that question before. Somehow I believe you really care. I thank you for that. Yes! Yes, I want to become a Christian. Will you help me?"

In each of these situations the love of God was expressed and faith was shared, but the way it was done varied greatly. Often we are tempted to approve and recommend only our favorite ways of witnessing and to disapprove of other methods without being aware that many ways are needed.

The word "pluralism" is used frequently today to describe the wide variety of stances, approaches, or viewpoints on any topic you can name. This book, with its rainbow of theological representations, may have its main strength in its pluralism. Thank God for each shade and hue.

Within the Church of the Brethren we have taken a special pride in our pluralism, which finds its basis in such time-honored principles as "no force in religion," and "the priesthood of all believers." There is the continual hope that we can be true to our own convictions while at the same time we affirm the other person or group who has some different convictions.

The same principle needs to be applied to evangelism. While we personally might advocate and practice one special kind of evangelism, other ways of sharing faith are equally valid and blessed by God.

Evangelism is telling the good news of God's love both in word and deed. But how do you convey that good news to a hostile, alienated gang of youth in the city? Developing a trust relationship through which to build lines of communication calls for both words and deeds. No amount of scriptural quotations or gospel words alone will build the trust relationship. The good news must be conveyed both in speech and action. We need all the imagination and creativity we can muster to express the good news of God's love. Therefore there is need for pluralism in ways to evangelize.

Revival meetings and evangelistic preaching missions are still valid, even for reaching unchurched people, if local church members are committed to contact neighbors and friends and invite them or bring them to church.

Visitation evangelism is a necessity because it has proven to be the most effective way of contacting unchurched people. Lay men and women calling on people in their homes to share God's love are a special and indispensable part of evangelism in the local church.

Small groups can be the church at its best. A caring, forgiving, affirming group which also deals with honest feelings of anger and fear and guilt can result in startling and thrilling spiritual growth. Small groups can help a person develop a close relationship with God, with self and with others. In such a setting faith is both shared and developed.

In similar ways, coffeehouses, youth clubs, human relations councils, relief and disaster projects, and whatever else you might dream of, could well offer valid ways to convey the good news of God's love.

Most congregations are eager to be more evangelistic. There are, however, times and situations where such a desire seems to be weak or even nonexistent. Perhaps there is a strong fear of taking into the Brethren fellowship too many non-Brethren who may not sufficiently appreciate or affirm our heritage or our ways of "running the church." Sometimes there is a fear that the front doors may swing open too wide. Yet, in spite of the exceptions, congregations seem genuinely eager to reach new people and to receive them into their fellowship and membership.

In the process of working with local churches

across the country, I have come to the conviction that there are two prerequisites to becoming an evangelistic congregation. One is a clear and solid relationship to God. The other is a freedom to celebrate that relationship. Without these two qualities or characteristics a local church will find evangelism attempts ineffective and unsuccessful.

An evangelistic church sends out invitations through human beings, for people to come both to a meaningful relationship with God in Christ and a meaningful relationship with people in the church fellowship. An invitation carries with it a promise. It would be an empty promise to send out invitations to a party when there is no party. Similarly it is inappropriate to send out invitations to participate in an exciting, enriching worship experience, to find and develop a firm relationship to God, and to encounter a loving, affirming fellowship, if there is little hope for fulfilling the implied promises.

To describe this concept I have developed a simple chart indicating three qualities of a healthy church (see page 131).

Before a local congregation can adequately be evangelistic there needs to be both a clear, strong relationship to God (faith) and a freedom to celebrate and rejoice in that faith. Of course all three qualities are ongoing growth experiences. We never fully achieve perfection in any of them, but seek to grow in all of them.

Quality number one means knowing who and whose we are. Some of the related concepts include:

- experiencing the good news of God's love

THREE QUALITIES OF A HEALTHY CHURCH

KNOWING	REJOICING	REACHING OUT
FAITH	**PRAISE**	**SERVICE AND WITNESS**
IDENTITY	CELEBRATION	EVANGELISM
Knowing who and whose we are Finding and experiencing salvation and assurance Relating successfully to God, to others, and to self Belonging to the company of the committed	Expressing personal and corporate joy Finding the freedom to share God's love Feeling God's spirit alive and moving Experiencing the peace and power of God	Responding to need Serving humanity Confronting and challenging persons, inviting their commitment Living out a life of love and care

- bringing our faith into focus (clear but not rigid)
- growing in a knowledge of the Bible
- developing a close, personal relationship to God
- making a life commitment to Christ and the Christian way
- finding assurance, confidence, salvation (present and future), meaning, and purpose
- working through the identity crises, a continual need
- having a strong, clear sense of mission, meaning that the local church knows what God has commissioned it to be and do

Quality number two expresses the need to let the "joy of our faith shine through." It includes concepts such as:

- finding freedom to express joy, personally and cooperately
- allowing the Spirit to move within our lives and within our corporate gatherings
- sharing faith freely in private conversation and public worship services
- making provision in our worship experiences for personal gifts to be given (gifts of talents, abilities, experiences, etc.)
- broadening the scope of what is acceptable in worship, testing it only with the question, "Will it assist people in worshiping God?"
- developing a loving, caring fellowship
- sensing a circle of prayer and spiritual power
- practicing the presence of God all the time.

If members of a congregation have a clear faith with a strong sense of mission, and if they have the freedom to celebrate and share that faith, then the third step of reaching out follows almost automatically. If someone is excited about what's happening at his church, the faith that is felt, the sense of God's call, and the joy of belonging to Christ and the church — then he will eagerly invite his neighbors and acquaintances, "Hey, how about coming with me?"

The third quality of a healthy church is one of reaching out, both in service and witness. It means sharing our faith in action and words. Related concepts include:

- experiencing and responding to the urge to reach out to others
- sensing and attempting to meet whatever human needs are evident
- caring for the earth and all of God's creation
- healing the brokenness, building bridges, developing caring and support systems
- sharing faith, inviting, confronting, and challenging others to make life commitments to God
- risking being vulnerable by getting involved, serving a cause, extending love
- applying faith to life, putting faith to the test

Each congregation can deal with the pre-requisites to evangelism — the *knowing* and *rejoicing* — by giving them conscious and deliberate attention. A local church can develop a sense of identity by intentionally discussing and deciding what its relationship to God is and what its mission is. A congregation can develop a strong, clear faith in Bible study groups, prayer meetings, theological discussion, and by freely sharing faith, person to person, in small groups and with the total congregation.

Likewise a congregation can grow surprisingly fast in the quality of rejoicing and praise. Admittedly some congregations find it difficult to "free-up" to the point where joy can actually be felt in the Sunday morning worship. It takes a little courage to experiment with new ways to give expression to God's truth and love and judgment, but any congregation can do it. A simple thing like sixty seconds of drama can bring a Bible story to life in a way that the congregation will never forget.

Both the knowing and rejoicing qualities can be developed rather quickly if there is deliberate planning for them. Then the third quality, evangelism, can also come alive.

The Great Commission is also our commission. Christ's words are for us: to go, to teach, to baptize. We can hear him say, "You shall be my witnesses in Pennsylvania, in Nebraska, in Tennessee, even to the uttermost parts of California."

We know full well the evangelism imperative. In our better moments we understand that faith, like love, is something that, if we give it away, we end up having more. And if we refuse to share it, we lose it. The urgency of sharing our faith is clear, and yet we hesitate. Why? Perhaps we don't know what we believe and therefore feel unable to share it. Perhaps our religious experience and our personal relationship to God isn't all that great that we are eager to tell others about it. Perhaps we are reluctant to share something so sacred and personal because of fear of rejection or ridicule.

There are two relatively quick ways to bring your faith into clear focus. One is to write down your convictions, and the second is to express them verbally. Once a person actually shares his faith he can dismiss the excuses he used to rely on.

I am inclined to believe it is a matter of deliberately making a decision and committing yourself to the task. It is like the old professor who near the end of his days confessed:

I have lived a toothless life;
I have never really bitten into anything;
I was saving myself for later on,
Only to realize too late,
My teeth are gone.

Before our teeth are gone, before it is too late, as individuals and congregations, we need to give ourselves fully to being witnesses for God. The whole world is awaiting the testimony. Call the witnesses!

Leland Wilson *is minister of the Church of the Brethren in La Verne, California. He previously served as director of the Department of Interpretation for the General Board of the Church of the Brethren and held pastorates in Kansas. At La Verne, one of the largest congregations of his denomination, he directs an extensive ministry to members of his own parish and to the community. He is also chairman of the American Committee of the World Friendship Center, Hiroshima, Japan. Leland Wilson has a particular interest in the life of Will Rogers, and has collected a large body of material by and about Rogers, such as books, newspaper and magazine articles, photographs, recording, and other memorabilia. He is married and is the father of three children.*

A Constant Invitation, a Continuing Response

Leland Wilson

"Why don't you give an invitation for Christ at the close of the Sunday service?" The question comes at times from visitors and also from members of the La Verne Church of the Brethren.

But we do. We do give an invitation. We give an invitation every time we gather for worship. And if there is no invitation, it is not by intent. It is by failure. It is by mistake.

When we speak of the hope that is experienced in the resurrection, we invite others to share in that experience. When we reflect, as Christians, upon the strength and the warmth of the fellowship in the church, we hope that others feel that warmth and that strength. When we proclaim the freedom we find in Jesus Christ, we extend an invitation to embrace that freedom. When the prophetic word is spoken concerning peace and justice, there is an invitation to action. When we explore the parable of the prodigal son, we note always that Father figure who runs to meet the son who is returning home. There has never been a more beautiful invitation than this.

So when someone asks, "Why don't we give an invitation?" we can only answer, "We do." And, then, we must continue the dialogue, for it is obvious that communication is incomplete. The invitataion has been given, but not in expected form.

Recently I received an invitation to a dinner. The card said R.S.V.P. and listed a telephone number. But the invitation that is usually present in our worship service does not carry a telephone number. It does not specify in one-two-three fashion the response that is to be made. It may be fair to say that in our worship we should sometimes become more explicit, more specific. Perhaps we should speak as concretely as Jesus did in inviting a rich young ruler to "sell all that you have and distribute to the poor."

There is another way in which we give the invitation each Sunday. It is with attendance sheets that are in the pews. These provide a place for persons to write their names and addresses. Along with other needs or interests they may indicate that they would like to become members of the church. This kind of invitation does not follow the sermon. Nor does it carry an emotional appeal. It may seem unlikely that anyone would

actually check his interest in becoming a member.
But people do! They do check, and several have
thus begun the process that has led them into
membership and fellowship in our congregation.

But the question, "Why don't you give an invitation?" is really not concerned with these kinds
of invitations. It is more specific than that. The
question is really, "Why don't you give an invitation following the sermon, for people to give their
hearts to Jesus Christ?" It is aimed at those who
have never been Christian. It is directed to those
who have drifted away — the heathen, the atheist,
the backslider, the sinner. Why don't we give an
invitation like Billy Graham, or some of the more
evangelistic churches?

First, it must be said that some in the Church
of the Brethren do give that kind of invitation.
They do so in revival meetings and sometimes on
Sunday mornings. Should we all give that kind
of invitation? The Scriptures seem to lend some
support to this idea. There was the day of Pentecost when Peter was preaching. Luke records in
the Acts of the Apostles, "So those who received
his word were baptized, and there were added that
day about three thousand souls" (Acts 2:41).
What an altar call! What a rush down front, as
Peter pleaded during the last chorus! Yet that is
not quite the way it happened. Peter related Jesus
of Nazareth to the words of the prophet Joel, and
to the words of King David. Peter spoke of the
meaning of the crucifixion. And that was his invitation.

The part of Peter's sermon that is preserved for us in the Scriptures carries only an implied invitation, but the people responded in a very explicit way. They began to ask, "Brethren, what shall we do?" (Acts 2:17-37). The sermon had been concluded. The preacher had moved out to the narthex. And the people who responded were asking not just Peter, but also the other apostles. When they sought direction, Peter said, "Repent, and be baptized every one of you in the name of Jesus Christ for the forgiveness of your sins; and you shall receive the gift of the Holy Spirit" (Acts 2:38).

Perhaps the longest sermon recorded in the Scriptures is that by Stephen. Certainly he had the power to stir the feelings of men. His testimony carried an invitation, and when the sermon was over, men were enraged. They rushed out and stoned him to death (Acts 7:1-60).

There was an immediate response by an Ethiopian eunuch to the opening of the Scriptures by Philip (Acts 8:26-40). But it was not a spur-of-the-moment thing. The eunuch had come to Jerusalem to worship. He was exploring the Scriptures. And there was considerable encounter between the two men before one baptized the other.

If there was ever an evangelist, it certainly was Paul. Whether he formed a specific invitation after his preaching is not clear. It *is* clear that people responded in different ways. Some became angry. Some went to sleep. But a very large number heard an invitation and helped to form the early church.

No, we cannot say that the Scriptures give us

clear guidance on how to present the invitation —
whether it should be explicit or whether it should
follow the sermon. But then, most of our worship
forms do not find clear specification in the Scriptures. They have emerged out of the common life
of the church and that revelation of God that was
given after his Book was completed.

When you ask why we don't give the kind of
invitation that is an emotional appeal following
the sermon, you pose a difficult question. I think
the answer lies in the character and life-style of
Brethren. So, to ask the question is like asking
why the family who reared me always found the
men going hunting on Thanksgiving. It's just that
it was a part of their living. If we wanted to do
so, however, we could probably trace ideas and
experiences that led them in that direction.

Giving a specific invitation at the close of the
sermon is a matter of life-style in faith. It is not
the kind of issue that we can resolve, saying that
one pattern is good, another bad, one pattern
right, another wrong. The invitation must be
given, but the way it is given reflects a life-style.
And the emotional appeal at the conclusion of a
service has simply not been the Brethren way.

BRETHREN were asking the question about the
invitation more than a hundred years ago. They
had seen the influence of the Wesleys. It looked
like the Methodists had a good thing going. Their
zeal to save and convert souls was amazingly effective, and the Methodists worked at nurturing the
newly converted. Some Brethren tried what they

saw their neighboring Christians doing. They even enjoyed some success at it, sweeping in a number of converts on a wave of enthusiasm. But something else went along with that. It was the problem of inactive members. The Annual Meeting of 1849 had before it a query asking, "What should be done with such members, as neglect attending our meetings for six or more months?"

In 1858 the Annual Meeting faced the invitation question head on. The query went like this: "How should Brethren proceed, after preaching, relative to getting members to join the church? Should the preacher, while singing a hymn, give an invitation to those who wish to join the church to come forward, or shall he leave it to them to make their own application?" The answer given by Annual Meeting was this: "Considered, that it is best to let them make their own application, as in Acts 2:37, and 16:30." The way of applying for membership in the church which was considered at one with Christian conversion, was to talk with the elders, to begin a period of serious reflection and study, and then receive the rite of baptism. The Annual Meetings in the 19th century gave frequent caution against revivals which they called "protracted meetings."

Why did we emerge with this kind of life-style in giving and responding to the invitation? It may be related to the persecution we have known, to the serious cost we have seen in discipleship. Because our faith has often brought us into conflict with the authorities and with our neighbors, because a changed life is expected in people, it may be that Brethren felt too much was involved to make a decision on the hearing of a sermon. It may be they felt a person really needs to have a "cooling off period" to consider the invitation.

These words come rolling out of Luke as a reminder: "For which of you, desiring to build a tower, does not first sit down and count the cost, whether he has enough to complete it? Otherwise, when he has laid a foundation, and is not able to finish, all who see it begin to mock him, saying, 'This man began to build, and was not able to finish'" (Luke 14:28-30).

Why did we emerge with this kind of life-style in giving and responding to the invitation? It may be related to the focus we give to living out our faith in everyday life. We have not tended to concentrate on that instant when a person says, "I do believe" for the first time.

The movies of earlier years and the fairy tales that deal with love usually portray it only in the context of courtship. Never marriage. The whole story gathers around the events that lead two people to each other. They make the commitment and then the curtain closes with the notation that "they lived happily ever after." They come to the point of commitment, but they do not show love growing. They do not show living out that commitment.

But reality of life suggests that courtship is actually a rather brief span and a rather limited expression of love. The fulfillment of love comes after the embrace of marriage. So faith finds its meaning and fulfillment, not in that time prior to the commitment, but in acting and living out the commitment.

There is something strangely appealing about an explicit invitation. I, too, like to hear one. And whenever I hear an invitation, I want to respond. Something within me wants to move. But really, I am not responding to the question exactly as it is put. For my response is not a completely new conversion, as it is not with many who respond to such an invitation. Many of those who go forward have done so often before, and will do so again. They are renewing their commitment, and in doing so, they are making their own adaptation of the evangelist's invitation.

There is another danger inherent in the implicit invitation. Fascination with our neighbor's style may make us deaf to the invitation which is given in our own style. By always wanting the invitation to be given to someone else, we may miss God's invitation to us.

If we take literally some worship forms, we might assume that once a person has accepted Christ as Savior, there is no further invitation, no further need to respond. But, strong as our interest in sharing the gospel may be, and in winning new people to Christ and his church, a mature faith would also keep in sight the need for continuing response. Perhaps one of the greatest needs of the church at this time is to develop ritual which calls for response from both the new and the renewed convert.

The invitation of Christ is always present. It must be faithfully extended in his name — he always asks for a response. True evangelism will be concerned that every opportunity be given to make that response meaningful and significant.